GOOD THINGS TO EAT

SUGGES ͟ ͟ BY RUFUS

A COLLECTION OF PRACTICAL RECIPES FOR
PREPARING MEATS, GAME, FOWL, FISH,
PUDDINGS, PASTRIES, ETC.

BY

RUFUS ESTES

In Facsimile with 56 Images
From the 1800s and Early 1900s
Illuminating Mr. Estes' Life and Time

Edited by D.J. Frienz

HOWLING AT THE MOON PRESS

Illustrations by Steve Quinn, Steve Quinn Creative Services, as noted

Book design by Tamara Dever, TLC Graphics, Orangevale, CA

10   9   8   7   6   5   4   3   2

ISBN# 0-9654333-1-5

Library of Congress Catalog Number: 99-60728

Publisher's Cataloging-in-Publication
    (provided by Quality Books, Inc.)

Estes, Rufus.
        Good things to eat, as suggested by Rufus ;
    a collection of practical recipes for preparing
    meats, game, fowl, fish, puddings, pastries, etc.
    / by Rufus Estes. -- 1st ed.
        p. cm.
        Includes index.
        LCCN: 99-60728
        ISBN: 0-9654333-1-5

        1. Cookery, American.   2. Railroads--Dining-car
    service--Miscellanea.   I. Title.

    TX715.E88 1999   641.5'76
                                    QBI99-230

Howl at the moon!
Celebrate that we are all part of each other
during this great adventure we call "life."

Howling at the Moon Press
P.O. Box 666
Jenks, OK   74037
E-mail: HATMPress@aol.com
On the World Wide Web: http://www.howling1.com

TO ORDER, CALL TOLL-FREE: 877-4-HOWLING

Printed in the U.S.A.

PUBLISHER'S NOTE:

Good Things To Eat was first published
in 1911 by the author, Mr. Rufus Estes.

The text of this edition of *Good Things
To Eat* is identical with the first printing.
Any "imperfections" such as typing errors,
misspellings, or inconsistencies in page
layout or chapter breaks occur just as the
original did. We believe they enhance the
book, just as an "imperfection" in a
fine fabric may enhance its texture and value.

Artwork is not identical to the 1911 edition.
Fifty-six photographs, illustrations, and food
advertisements from the late 1800s and early
1900s have been added to help illuminate
Mr. Estes' life and culinary times. Mr. Estes'
photograph on the front cover and 2nd page,
the illustration of the lamp on the original
title page, and the illustration of the letter
"T" on the Forward are original and
from the 1911 edition.

*In remembrance of the great cooks
who penciled in the margins of this book,
splattered it with grease, and passed
it down to me — Susan Mary Greenleaf
Jones, Nora Bell Downs Greenleaf,
and Susan Monday Downs. And in
remembrance of the great chef who has lead
4 generations of my family through many
wonderful meals, Mr. Rufus Estes.*

MANY, MANY THANKS TO the Afrigenese Web site, Elsa Altshool, Cleone Black, Mike Blechner, Jerry Borofsky, Joe Carlin, Chicago Historical Society, Sandi Craighead, Tamara Dever, Alicia Diehl, Bob Glancy, Mark Graziano, Springfield Rieffel Homachek, Kathleen Johnson, Jamie Jordan, Gary and Yvonne Jones and their family, Library of Congress archives, Bryan Logan, Brad Luna, Metropolitan Archives of Nashville and Davidson County Tennessee, Lea Pierce, Project GenWeb, Pullman archives and the Newberry Library of Chicago, Steve Quinn, Lloyd Rich – Attorney At Law, Sapulpa Public Library, Meg Savilonis, Chip Seay, Bob Skilnik, Tina Twilley, Larry Twilley, USGenWeb project, especially People of Color in Old Tennessee from the TNGebWeb Project, Rick Wellington, Mary Westheimer, and Elizabeth White.

INTRODUCTION

A Word From The Editor

What do we really know about the life of chef Rufus Estes?

He lived an exceptional life in fascinating but difficult times. His hand penned one of too-few first-hand accounts of what it was like to be a little boy and a slave during the Civil War. And, in many ways, his story reflects what was golden and good about the westward movement of America.

Mr. Estes migrated, as many did, for opportunities. From his risks and hard labor, he achieved greatness. He became the creme de la creme of Pullman Private Car attendants. He, in his words, "cared for" two presidents ... Grover Cleveland and Benjamin Harrison. He also "cared for" European royalty and the most celebrated actors, musicians, and explorers of his day.

More important than Mr. Estes' association with the famous, perhaps, is how well Mr. Estes "cared for" his widowed mother during her life, taking her with him to Chicago.

While Mr. Estes tells us much about his life, he omits much, too. The ugliness of the Pullman strike, an early marriage, the dangerous working conditions of the railroads, and the hardships he endured. In fact, what Mr. Estes leaves out of this book reveals more about his character, nobleness, and style than much of what he shares.

What does he include? Almost two pages on the nameless captains of industry he "cared for" who became his friends and the inspiration he needed to write this book.

After months of research, we haven't been able to gather all the facts of Mr. Estes amazing life. Perhaps we never will. But here's what we do know. His voice rings strong and true throughout this book.

Listen, as you read, and you may hear the rush of train tracks under your feet as a fat canvas-back duck roasts in a brisk oven. Inhale deeply and the sweet heavy fragrance of a creamy southern magnolia or the thick expensive leather from the prestigious Black republican social club Mr. Estes lived above, the Appomattox, may be yours. Close your eyes and gentler times, when a man could candy a violet or "crystallize" a cowslip might not seem like so long ago.

And, if you will, as you read these recipes, please remember the great man hurriedly jotting down recipes as a wooden train car rocks through the night and a cranky diva on a diet practices her scales in the next room.

You see, Mr. Estes' life is not the details we found or didn't find in mounds of yellowed papers and microfiche. His life is in what he loved ... his food, these recipes, and the people he "cared for" and dedicated this book to.

D.J. Frienz

CHAPTERS

GOOD THINGS TO EAT

As Suggested By

RUFUS

COVER FROM 1911 EDITION OF
Good Things To Eat

GOOD THINGS TO EAT

AS

SUGGESTED BY RUFUS

A COLLECTION OF PRACTICAL RECIPES FOR
PREPARING MEATS, GAME, FOWL, FISH,
PUDDINGS, PASTRIES, ETC.

BY

RUFUS ESTES

FORMERLY OF THE PULLMAN COMPANY PRIVATE CAR SERVICE, AND PRESENT
CHEF OF THE SUBSIDIARY COMPANIES OF THE UNITED STATES
STEEL CORPORATIONS IN CHICAGO

CHICAGO
PUBLISHED BY THE AUTHOR
1911

FOREWORD

THAT the average parent is blind to the faults of its offspring is a fact so obvious that in attempting to prove or controvert it time and logic are both wasted. Ill temper in a child is, alas! too often mistaken for an indication of genius; and impudence is sometimes regarded as a sign of precocity

The author, however, has honestly striven to avoid this common prejudice. This book, the child of his brain, and experience, extending over a long period of time and varying environment, he frankly admits is not without its faults —is far from perfect; but he is satisfied that, notwithstanding its apparent shortcomings, it will serve in a humble way some useful purpose.

The recipes given in the following pages represent the labor of years. Their worth has been demonstrated, not experimentally, but by actual tests, day by day and month by month, under dissimilar, and, in many instances, not too favorable conditions.

One of the pleasures in life to the normal man is good eating, and if it be true that real happiness consists in making others happy, the author can at least feel a sense of gratification in the thought that his attempts to satisfy the cravings of the inner man have not been wholly unappreciated by the many that he has had the pleasure of serving—-some of whom are now his stanchest friends. In fact, it was in response to the insistence and encouragement of these friends that he embarked in the rather hazardous undertaking of offering this collection to a discriminating public

To snatch from his daily toil a few moments, here and there, in order to arrange with some degree of symmetry, not the delicacies that would awaken the jaded appetite of the gourmet, but to prepare an ensemble that might, with equal grace, adorn the home table or banquet board, has proven a task of no mean proportions. Encouraged by his friends, however, he persevered and this volume is the results of his effort.

If, when gathered around the festal board, in camp or by fireside, on train or ship, "trying out" the recipes, his friends will pause, retrospectively, and with kindly feelings think from whence some of the good things emanated, the author will feel amply compensated for the care, the thought, the labor he has expended in the preparation of the book; and to those friends, individually and collectively, it is therefore dedicated.

SKETCH OF MY LIFE

I was born in Murray County, Tennessee, in 1857, a slave. I was given the name of my master, D. J. Estes, who owned my mother's family, consisting of seven boys and two girls, I being the youngest of the family.

After the war broke out all the male slaves in the neighborhood for miles around ran off and joined the "Yankees." This left us little folks to bear the burdens. At the age of five I had to carry water from the spring about a quarter of a mile from the house, drive the cows to and from the pastures, mind the calves, gather chips, etc.

In 1867 my mother moved to Nashville, Tennessee, my grandmother's home, where I attended one term of school. Two of my brothers were lost in the war, a fact that wrecked my mother's health somewhat and I thought I could be of better service to her and prolong her life by getting work. When summer came I got work milking cows for some neighbors, for which I got two dollars a month. I also carried hot dinners for the laborers in the fields, for which each one paid me twenty-five cents per month. All of this, of course, went to my mother. I worked at different places until I was sixteen years old, but long before that time I was taking care of my mother.

At the age of sixteen I was employed in Nashville by a restaurant-keeper named Hemphill. I worked there until I was twenty-one years of age. In 1881 I came to Chicago and got a position at 77 Clark Street, where I remained for two years at a salary of ten dollars a week.

In 1883 I entered the Pullman service, my first superintendent being J. P. Mehen. I remained in their service until 1897. During the time I was in their service some of the most prominent people in the world traveled in the car assigned to me, as I was selected to handle all special parties. Among the distinguished people who traveled in my care were Stanley, the African explorer; President Cleveland; President Harrison; Adelina Patti, the noted singer of the world at that time; Booth and Barrett. Modjeski and Paderewski. I also had charge of the car for Princess Eulalie of Spain, when she was the guest of Chicago during the World's Fair.

In 1894 I set sail from Vancouver on the Empress of China with Mr. and Mrs. Nathan A. Baldwin for Japan, visiting the Cherry Blossom Festival at Tokio.

In 1897 Mr. Arthur Stillwell, at that time president of the Kansas City, Pittsburg & Gould Railroad, gave me charge of his magnificent $20,000 private car. I remained with him seventeen months when the road went into the hands of receivers, and the car was sold to John W. Gates syndicate. However, I had charge of the car under the new management until 1907, since which time I have been employed as chef of the subsidiary companies of the United States Steel Corporation in Chicago.

Celebrity pianist Ignace Ian Paderewski (1860 – 1941), his entourage, and, quite possibly, cookbook author Rufus Estes (sitting center) aboard Paderewski's private car, the General Stanley. Paderewski later became prime minister of Poland.

ILLUSTRATION BY STEVE QUINN

When faced with the depression of 1893, George M. Pullman, builder of the luxurious railroad cars Rufus Estes worked on between 1883 & 1897, laid off some employees and cut the salaries of others 19%. A year later, when Pullman refused to reinstate salaries even after he posted earnings, a bitter strike under the leadership of Eugene V. Debs ensued. To keep the mail running and end the violence, President Cleveland sent four companies of the Fifteenth Infantry plus 2,000 regulars into Chicago.

ILLUSTRATION BY STEVE QUINN

Mr. Rufus Estes "took care of" Grover Cleveland (1837–1908), when the 22nd and 24th president of the United States traveled a la Pullman. Although Cleveland was sometimes nicknamed "Grover the Good" because he fought against Republican and Democratic wrong-doing as Governor of New York, his decision to send troops into Chicago during the Pullman strike was controversial. Early in his career he was an attorney for the railroad.

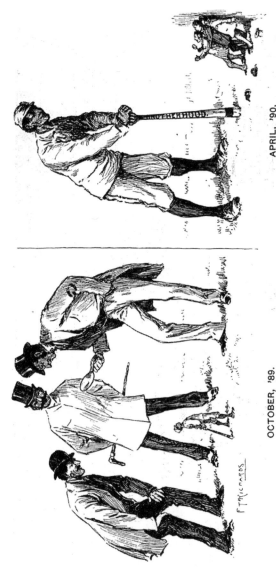

OCTOBER, '89.

Chorus of League Magnates: "WHAT IS THIS AMUSING LITTLE OBJECT."

APRIL, '90.

"GREAT SCOTT! WHO'D A THOUGHT IT WOULD GROW SO BIG IN THIS LITTLE TIME?"

From Life magazine (April 3, 1890).

Whether you call him the "Barbed Wire King," a progenitor of U. S. Steel, or "Bet-A-Million," as he was best known, John Warne Gates (1855 – 1911) was a colorful man, famous gambler, and Mr. Rufus Estes' employer from 1898 until 1907.

Leaded glass, fine hand-carved wood cabinetry, and velvet upholstery adorn the private car Mr. Estes was responsible for from 1898 until 1907. The organ (left) was installed for Arthur E. Stillwell, builder of the Kansas City, Pittsburgh & Gulf Railway and founder of Port Arthur, Texas. Mr. Stillwell was a religious man, and he used the organ on Sunday mornings for church services held in the car. What gambler Bet-A-Million Gates used the organ for, however, is purely speculation.

ILLUSTRATIONS THIS PAGE BY STEVE QUINN.

Over 186,000 miles of
railroad tracks were laid
between 1850 and 1890
(pictured above),
when tracks spread over
195,000 miles of U.S. soil.

Trains from the 1800's and early 1900's look charming, but were,
in fact, quite treacherous. In 1888, 2,070 men were killed at work,
and 20,148 were injured.

ILLUSTRATION BY STEVE QUINN

Nº 1162. *Empress Ship.*

Thompson's Studio, Vancouver. B.C.

*In 1894, the Empress of China steamliner (above)
took Mr. Estes from Vancouver to Tokyo in about 30 days.*

Sohmer used the face of the most celebrated coloratura soprana
of the 19th century, Adelina Patti (1843-1919), to sell pianos.
The author of this cookbook, Rufus Estes, took care of
Ms. Patti, quite possibly on her private car, the Adelina Patti.
Ms. Patti's private "boudoir" car caused almost as much of
a sensation as she did. It was lavishly decorated by
Parisian artists to the tune of $30,000 in 1884 dollars.

RUFUS ESTES, NOW AN AUTHOR

Writes Book on "Things Good to Eat
Mr. Rufus Estes, Interne at Appomattox...
mattox Club, one of Chicago's famil...
lar char... known chefs of Chicago...
pleted his book entitled "Good
Things to Eat,"...
under...

CHICAGO DEFENDER

Saturday May 6, 1911

RUFUS ESTES,
NOW AN AUTHOR

Writes Book on "Things Good to Eat"

Mr. Rufus Estes, Interne at Appomattox Club, one of Chicago's familiar characters and one of the best known chefs of Chicago, has completed his book entitled "Good Things to Eat," which he has had under construction for more than ten years. The first book that was received from the publishers, which contained the author's autograph, was auctioned off to the highest bidder in the offices of the Illinois Steel Company, where Mr. Estes is employed. After some lively bidding, the assistant secretary of the company proved to be the highest bidder at $11, and was the recipient of the first book.

1910 Postcard of Chicago's State Street at noon.

HINTS TO KITCHEN MAIDS

It is always necessary to keep your kitchen in the best condition.

Breakfast—If a percolator is used it should first be put into operation. If the breakfast consists of grapefruit, cereals, etc., your cereal should be the next article prepared. If there is no diningroom maid, you can then put your diningroom in order. If hot bread is to be served (including cakes) that is the next thing to be prepared. Your gas range is of course lighted, and your oven heated. Perhaps you have for breakfast poached eggs on toast, Deerfoot sausage or boiled ham. One of the above, with your other dishes, is enough for a person employed indoors.

When your breakfast gong is sounded put your biscuits, eggs, bread, etc., in the oven so that they may be ready to serve when the family have eaten their grapefruit and cereal.

Luncheon—This is the easiest meal of the three to prepare. Yesterday's dinner perhaps consisted of roast turkey, beef or lamb, and there is some meat left over; then pick out one of my receipts calling for minced or creamed meats; baked or stuffed potatoes are always nice, or there may be cold potatoes left over that can be mashed, made into cakes and fried.

Dinner—For a roast beef dinner serve vegetable soup as the first course, with a relish of vegetables in season and horseradish or chow-chow pickle, unless you serve salad.

If quail or ducks are to be served for dinner, an old Indian dish, wild rice, is very desirable. Prepare this rice as follows:

Place in a double boiler a cupful of milk or cream to each cupful of rice and add salt and pepper to taste. It requires a little longer to cook than the ordinary rice, but must not be stirred. If it becomes dry add a little milk from time to time.

Do not serve dishes at the same meal that conflict. For instance, if you have sliced tomatoes, do not serve tomato soup. If, however, you have potato soup, it would not be out of place to serve potatoes with your dinner.

Fish should never be served without a salad of some kind.

The above are merely suggestions that have been of material assistance to me.

TABLE OF WEIGHTS AND MEASURES

Four teaspoonfuls of a liquid equal 1 tablespoonful.
Four tablespoonfuls of a liquid equal ½ gill or ¼ cup.
One-half cup equals 1 gill.
Two gills equal 1 cup.
Two cups equal 1 pint.
Two pints (4 cups) equal 1 quart.
Four cups of flour equal 1 pound or 1 quart.
Two cups of butter, solid, equal 1 pound.
One half cup of butter, solid, equals ¼ pound 4 ounces.
Two cups of granulated sugar equal 1 pound.
Two and one half cups of powdered sugar equal 1 pound.
One pint of milk or water equals 1 pound.
One pint of chopped meat equals 1 pound.
Ten eggs, shelled, equal 1 pound.
Eight eggs with shells equal 1 pound.
Two tablespoonfuls of butter equal 1 ounce.
Two tablespoonfuls of granulated sugar equal 1 ounce.
Four tablespoonfuls of flour equal 1 ounce.
Four tablespoonfuls of coffee equal 1 ounce.
One tablespoonful of liquid equals ½ ounce.
Four tablespoonfuls of butter equal 2 ounces or ¼ cup.
All measurements are level unless otherwise stated in the recipe.

GOOD THINGS TO EAT

SOUPS

ASPARAGUS SOUP—Take three pounds of knuckle of veal and put it to boil in a gallon of water with a couple of bunches of asparagus, boil for three hours, strain, and return the juice to the pot. Add another bunch of asparagus, chopped fine, and boil for twenty minutes, mix a tablespoonful of flour in a cup of milk and add to the soup. Season with salt and pepper, let it come to a boil, and serve at once.

BEAN SOUP—One-half pound or one cup is sufficient for one quart of soup. Soups can be made which use milk or cream as basis. Any kind of green vegetable can be used with them, as creamed celery or creamed cauliflower. The vegetable is cooked and part milk and part water or part milk and part cream are used.

BISQUE OF CLAMS—Place a knuckle of veal, weighing about a pound and one-half, into a soup kettle, with a quart of water, one small onion, a sprig of parsley, a bay leaf, and the liquor drained from the clams, and simmer gradually for an hour and a half, skimming from time to time; strain the soup and again place it in the kettle; rub a couple of tablespoonfuls of butter with an equal amount of flour together and add it to the soup when it is boiling, stirring until again boiling; chop up twenty-five clams very fine, then place them in the soup, season and boil for about five minutes, then add a pint of milk or cream, and remove from the fire immediately, and serve.

BISQUE OF LOBSTER—Remove the meat of the lobster from its shell and cut the tender pieces into quarter-inch dice; put the ends of the claw-meat and any tough portions in a saucepan with the bones of the body and a little cold water and boil for twenty minutes, adding a little water from time to time as may be necessary; put the coral to dry in a moderate oven, and mix a little flour with some cold milk, and stir the milk, which should be boiling, stirring over the fire for ten

11

minutes, then strain the water from the bones and other parts, mix it with milk, add a little butter, salt, pepper and cayenne to taste, and rub the dry coral through a fine-haired sieve, putting enough into the soup having it a bright pink color. Place the grease fat and lobster dice in a soup tureen, strain the boiling soup over them, and serve at once.

BISQUE OF OYSTERS—Place about thirty medium-sized oysters in a saucepan together with their own juice and poach them over a hot fire, after which drain well; then fry a shallot colorless in some butter, together with an onion, sprinkle over them a little curry and add some of the oyster juice, seasoning with salt and red pepper. Pound the oysters to a good firm paste, moistening them with a little of their juice, and strain through fine tammy cloth. Warm them over the fire, but do not let them boil; add a small quantity of thickening of potato flour mixed with a little water. When about to serve incorporate some cream and fine butter, garnishing with some chopped oysters and mushrooms, mixed with breadcrumbs and herbs. Add a little seasoning of salt, pepper and nutmeg, some raw egg yolks, and roll this mixture into ball-shape pieces, place them on a well-buttered baking sheet in a slack oven and poach them, then serve.

BLACK BEAN SOUP—Wash one pint of black beans, cover with one quart of cold water and let soak over night. In the morning pour off the water and pour over three pints of cold water. Cook, covered, until tender, four or five hours, add one tablespoonful of salt the last hour, rub through a strainer, add the strained beans to the water in which they were boiled, return to the soup kettle. Melt one tablespoonful of flour, stir this into the hot soup, let boil, stirring constantly; add a little pepper, slice thinly one lemon, put all the slices into the tureen and pour the soup over. Serve very hot.

CHESTNUT SOUP—Peel and blanch the chestnuts, boil them in salted water until quite soft, pass through a sieve, add more water if too thick, and a spoonful of butter or several of sweet cream. Season to taste and serve with small squares of bread fried crisp in butter or olive oil.

CHICKEN GUMBO, CREOLE STYLE—For about twelve or fifteen, one young hen chicken, half pound ham, quart fresh okra, three large tomatoes, two onions, one kernel garlic, one small red pepper, two tablespoons flour, three quarts boiling water, half pound butter, one bay leaf, pinch salt and cayenne pepper. To mix, mince your ham, put in the bottom of an iron kettle if preferred with the above ingredients except the chicken. Clean and cut your chicken up and put in separate saucepan with about a quart or more of water and teaspoonful of salt; set to the side of the fire for about an hour; skim when necessary. When the chicken is thoroughly done strip the meat from the bone and mix both together; just before serving add a quart of shrimps.

CREAM OF CELERY SOUP—Chop fine one head of celery and put on to cook in one pint of water. Boil until tender, add one pint of milk, thicken with a spoonful of butter, season to taste, and strain. Then add one cupful of whipped cream and serve at once.

EGG SOUP—Beat three eggs until light, then add one-half cupful of thick sweet cream and one cupful of milk, pour over this two quarts of boiling water, set on the fire until it comes to a boil, season to taste, then pour over broken bread in the tureen and serve.

GREEN PEA SOUP—Put one quart of green peas into two cups of boiling water, add a saltspoon of salt, and cook until tender. Rub peas and liquor through a puree strainer, add two cups of boiling water, and set back where the pulp will keep hot. Heat two cups of milk, add a teaspoon of flour rubbed into a rounding tablespoon of butter, season with salt, pepper, and a level teaspoon of sugar. Add to the hot vegetable pulp, heat to the boiling point, and serve.

GREEN TOMATO SOUP—Chop fine five green tomatoes and boil twenty minutes in water to cover. Then add one quart hot milk, to which a teaspoonful soda has been added, let come to a boil, take from the fire and add a quarter cupful butter rubber into four crackers rolled fine, with salt and pepper to taste.

ONION SOUP—Cut three onions small, put one-quarter cup of butter in a kettle and toast one tablespoon flour till bright yellow in color; in it mix with this the onions, pour on as much broth as is wanted, add a little mace and let boil, then strain, allow to cook a little longer, add yolk of two eggs, and serve.

PEANUT SOUP—Made like a dry pea soup. Soak a pint and one-half nut meats over night in two quarts of water. In the morning add three quarts of bayleaf, stalk of celery, blade of mace and one slice of onion. Boil slowly for four or five hours, stirring frequently to keep from burning. Rub through a sieve and return to the fire, when heated through again add one cupful of cream. Serve hot with croutons.

SAGO SOUP—Wash one-half cup sago in warm water, add desired amount of boiling broth (meat or chicken), a little mace and cook until the sago is soft, and serve.

SALMON SOUP—Take the skin and bones from canned salmon and drain off the oil. Chop fine enough of the fish to measure two-thirds of a cup. Cook a thick slice of onion in a quart of milk twenty minutes in a double boiler. Thicken with one-quarter cup of flour rubbed smooth with one rounding tablespoonful of butter. Cook ten minutes, take out the onion, add a saltspoon of pepper, one level teaspoon of salt and the salmon. Rub all through a fine strainer, and serve hot. The amount of salmon may be varied according to taste.

SORREL SOUP—Wash thoroughly a pint of sorrel leaves and put in a saucepan with two tablespoonfuls of butter, four or five of the large outside leaves, a sliced onion, and a few small sprigs of parsley. Toss over the fire for a few minutes, then sift into the pan two tablespoonfuls of flour and stir until blended with the butter remaining. Transfer to the soup kettle and pour in gradually stirring all the time, three quarts of boiling water. Cook gently for fifteen or twenty minutes, then add a cupful of mashed potato and one of hot milk. Season with salt, pepper and a little nutmeg. Have in the soup tureen some croutons of bread toasted brown, pour the hot soup over them and serve. The sorrel should be cut in fine pieces before cooking. This is one of delicacies of the early spring, its slightly acid flavor making it particularly appetizing.

TOMATO SOUP—Put one quart can of tomatoes, two cups of water, one-half level tablespoon of sugar, one level teaspoon of salt, four whole cloves, and four peppercorns together in a saucepan and simmer twenty minutes. Fry a rounding tablespoon of chopped onion and half as much minced parsley in a rounding tablespoon of butter until yellow; add two level tablespoons of cornstarch. Stir until smooth, then turn into the boiling soup and simmer ten minutes. Add more salt and pepper and strain.

TOMATO SOUP—Into a saucepan put one quart can of tomatoes and two cups of broth from soup bones. To make this cover the bones and meat with cold water and simmer slowly for several hours. Add to tomato and stock a bit of bay leaf one stalk celery cut in pieces, six peppercorns, a level teaspoon of salt and a rounding teaspoon of sugar. Cook slowly until tomato is soft. Meanwhile put a rounding tablespoon of butter in a small saucepan and when melted and hot turn in a medium-sized onion cut fine. When this has cooked slowly until yellow, but not browned, add enough of the tomato to dilute it, then turn all back into the larger saucepan. Mix and press through a strainer to take out the seeds and lots of vegetables, reheat, and serve with small croutons.

TOMATO SOUP, CORNED BEEF STOCK—Put one quart can tomatoes on to boil, add six peppercorns, one-half inch blade of mace and a bit of bay leaf the same size. Fry one sliced onion in one level tablespoonful butter or beef fat until slightly colored, add this to the tomato, and simmer until the tomato is quite soft, and the liquor reduced one-half. Stir in one-fourth teaspoon of soda, and when it stops foaming turn into a puree strainer and rub the pulp through. Put the strained tomato on to boil again and add an equal amount of corned beef liquor or enough to make three pints in all.

Melt one heaped tablespoon butter in a smooth saucepan, add one heaped tablespoon cornstarch, and gradually add part of the boiling soup. Stir as it thickens, and when smooth stir this into the remainder of the soup. Add one teaspoon salt and one-fourth teaspoon paprika. Reserve one pint of this soup to use with spaghetti. Serve buttered and browned crackers with the soup.

VEGETABLE BROTH—Take turnips, carrots, potatoes, beets, celery, all, or two or three, and chop real fine. Then mix with them an equal amount of cold water, put in a kettle, just bring to a boil, not allowing it to boil for about three or four hours, and then drain off the water. The flavor will be gone from the vegetables and will be in the broth.

VEGETABLE SOUP—Take one-half a turnip, two carrots, three potatoes, three onions and a little cabbage. Run through a meat chopper with coarse cutter and put to cook in cold water. Cook about three hours. If you wish you can put a little bit of cooking oil in. When cooked add one quart of tomatoes. This will need about six quarts of water.

The most nutritious soups are made from peas and beans.

VEGETABLE SOUP (without stock)—One-half cup each of carrot and turnip, cut into small pieces, three-fourths cup of celery, cut fine, one very small onion sliced thin, four level table-spoons of butter, three-fourths cup of potato, cut into small dice, one and one-half quarts of boiling water, salt and pepper to taste. Prepare the vegetables and cook the carrot, celery and onion in the butter for ten minutes without browning. Add the potato and cook for three minutes longer, then add the water and cook slowly for one hour. Rub through a sieve, add salt and pepper to taste, and a little buter if desired.

WHITE SOUP—Put six pounds of lean gravy beef into a saucepan, with half gallon of water and stew gently until all the good is extracted and remove beef. Add to the liquor six pounds of knuckle of veal, one-fourth pound ham, four onions, four heads of celery, cut into small pieces, a few peppercorns and bunch of sweet herbs. Stew gently for seven or eight hours, skimming off the fat as it rises to the top. Mix with the crumbs of two French rolls two ounces of blanched sweet almonds and put in a saucepan with a pint of cream and a little stock, boil ten minutes, then pass through a silk sieve, using a wooden spoon in the process. Mix the cream and almonds with the soup, turn into a tureen, and serve.

WINE SOUP—Put the yolks of twelve eggs and whites of six in an enameled saucepan and beat thoroughly. Pour in one and a half breakfast cupfuls of water, add six ounces of loaf sugar, the grated rind and strained juice of a large lemon, one and one-half pints of white wine. Whisk the soup over a gentle fire until on the point of boiling, removing immediately. Turn into a tureen, and serve with a plate of sponge cakes or fancy biscuits. (This soup should be served as soon as taken from fire.)

CHESTNUT SOUP—Peel and blanch the chestnuts, boil them in salted water until quite soft, pass through a sieve, add more water if too thick, and a spoonful of butter or several of sweet cream, season to taste, and serve with small squares of bread fried crisp in butter or olive oil.

CATCHING SMELTS AT   SUMMERSIDE, P. E. I.

Photo by W. S. Louson   Garden of the Gulf Series 2691 S

CATCHING SMELTS AT SUMMERSIDE, P.E.I.

Photo by W. S. Louson was made into a postcard and mailed to Massachusetts from Toronto, Canada in 1909.

Buying clams from a street vendor in Mulberry Bend, New York, circa 1900.

Photograph courtesy of the Library of Congress.

FISH

BOILED CODFISH, WITH CREAM SAUCE—Take out the inside of a cod by the white skin of the belly, taking care to remove all blood. Place the fish in a kettle with salted cold water; boil fast at first, then slowly. When done take out and skin. Pour over it a sauce made as follows:

One-fourth pound butter put into a stewpan with one tablespoonful of flour, moistened with one pint of cream or rich milk, and salt and pepper, and also one teaspoonful essence of anchovies. Place the pan over the fire and let thicken, but not boil.

BOILED MACKEREL—Prepare and clean some mackerel. Put in water and boil until they are done. When cooked, drain and put the mackerel on a hot dish. Blanch some fennel in salted water. When it is soft drain and chop finely. Put one tablespoonful in half pint of butter sauce. Serve in a sauce boat with the fish.

BOILED SALMON WITH SAUCE TARTARE—Scrape the skin of the fish, wipe, and if you have no regular fish kettle with a perforated lid, tie in a piece of cheesecloth and place gently in a kettle of boiling salted water. Push the kettle back on the fire (where it will simmer gently, instead of boiling hard) and cook, allowing about six minutes to the pound. Remove carefully, drain, and chill. If the fish breaks and looks badly take out the bones, flake, pile lightly on the platter and pour the sauce over it. This may be a hot sauce Hollandaise or a cold sauce tartare.

BROILED MACKEREL—Draw and wash the mackerel. Cut off heads and rub over with salt and leave for an hour. Rub a gridiron with olive oil, lay the mackerel on it and broil over a charcoal fire. Place some chopped parsley and onions on a hot dish, with the hot fish, squeezing over the mackerel a little lemon juice. Serve hot.

BROILED MACKEREL, WITH BLACK BUTTER—Take some mackerel, open and remove bones. Season with butter, pepper, and salt. Place the fish on a gridiron and broil over a clear fire. Put a part of the butter in a saucepan and stir it over the fire until it is richly browned, squeezing into it a little lemon juice. Place the fish on a hot dish, arrange some sprigs of parsley around it, and pour over it the butter sauce, and serve hot.

CODFISH CONES—When it is not convenient to make and fry fish balls try this substitute. Pick enough salt codfish into shreds to measure two cups and let stand in cold water for two or more hours, then drain dry. Make a sauce from one cup of hot milk, two level tablespoons each of flour and butter, and cook five minutes. Mash and season enough hot boiled potatoes to measure two cups, add the sauce and the fish and beat well with a fork. Shape in small cones, set on a butter pan, brush with melted butter and scatter fine bread crumbs over. Set in oven to brown.

CODFISH HASH—Take a cup of cooked cod, pick in pieces and soak in cold water for twelve hours. Boil some potatoes and add them to the finely chopped fish, a little at a time. Put in a saucepan with some butter and stir. Let it cook gently.

FINNAN HADDIE FISH CAKES—The finnan haddie parboiled with an equal quantity of mashed potatoes, season with melted butter, salt and pepper, add a beaten egg, and mold into cakes.

FISH, EAST INDIA STYLE—Peel two medium-sized onions, cut into thin slices. Put in a stewpan with a small lump of butter and fry until lightly browned. Pour over them some white stock, judging the quantity by that of the fish; one ounce of butter, little curry powder, salt, lemon juice, a little sugar, and cayenne pepper. Boil the stock for fifteen or twenty minutes, then strain into a stewpan, skim and put in the fish, having it carefully prepared. Boil gently, without breaking the fish. Wash and boil half a cup of rice in water, and when cooked it should be dried and the grains unbroken. Turn the curry out on a hot dish, garnish with croutons of fried bread. Serve hot, with the rice in separate dish.

FISH EN CASSEROLE—One of those earthen baking dishes with close-fitting cover of the same ware and fit for placing on the table is especially useful for cooking fish. For instance, take two pounds of the thick part of cod or haddock, both of which are cheap fish. Take off the skin and lay in the casserole. Make a sauce from two cups of milk heated, with a good slice of onion, a rounding tablespoon of minced parsley, a small piece of mace, a few gratings of the yellow rind of lemon, half a level teaspoon of salt, and a little white pepper. Cook in the top of a double boiler for twenty minutes. Heat one-quarter cup of butter in a saucepan, add three level tablespoons of flour, and cook smooth, turn on the hot milk after straining out the season-ings. Cook until thick and pour over the fish. Cover and bake half hour, then if the fish is done serve in the same dish with little finely minced parsley scattered over.

LOUISIANA COD—Melt one-quarter cup of butter and let it begin to color, add two level tablespoons of flour and stir until smooth. Add one cup of water and cook five minutes. Add half a level teaspoon of salt, half as much pepper, and a teaspoon of lemon juice. Chop fine one medium-size onion and one small green pepper, after taking out the seeds. Brown them in two tablespoons of butter, add one cup of strained tomatoes, a bit of bay leaf, and the prepared sauce. Put slices of cod cut an inch thick into a casserole, pour on the sauce, cover closely, and bake in a slow oven three-quarters of an hour.

METELOTE OF HADDOCK—Wash and skin the haddock and remove the flesh from the bones in firm pieces suitable for serving. Put the head, bones and trimmings to cook in cold water and add a small sliced onion and salt and pepper. Boil six good-sized onions until tender, then drain and slice and put half of them into a buttered baking dish. Arrange the pieces of fish on these, sprinkle with salt and pepper, then add the remaining onions. Drain the fish from the trimmings, add to it two tablespoons lemon juice and pour it over onions and fish. Cover very closely and cook in the oven until the fish is tender. Then drain off the liquid, beat it to the boiling point, and thicken it with two eggs slightly beaten and diluted with a little of the hot liquid. Arrange the onions on a hot platter and place the fish on top, then pour over the thickened liquid.

A MOLD OF SALMON—If where one cannot get fresh fish, the canned salmon makes a delicious mold. Serve very cold on a bed of crisp lettuce or cress. Drain off the juice from a can of salmon, and flake, picking out every fragment of bone and skin. Mix with the fish one egg lightly beaten, the juice of a half lemon, a cup fine dry bread crumbs, and salt and pepper to season. Pack in a buttered mold which has a tight-fitting tin cover, steam for two hours, and cool. After it gets quite cold set on the ice until ready to carve.

OYSTERS A LA POULETTE—One quart oysters, four level tablespoons butter, four level tablespoons flour, one-half level teaspoon salt, one-fourth level teaspoon celery salt, one-half cup oysters liquor, one cup each of chicken stock and milk, juice one-half lemon. Look over the oysters, heat quickly to the boiling point, then drain and strain the liquor through cheesecloth. Melt the butter, add the flour, salt and celery salt, and when blended add the oyster liquor, chicken stock and milk, stirring until thick and smooth. Cook for five minutes, then add the oysters and lemon juice, and serve at once.

OYSTER FRICASSE—Put one pint of oysters into a double boiler or into the top of the chafing dish. As soon as the edges curl add the slightly beaten yolks of three eggs, a few grain of pepper and half a teaspoon of salt. Set over hot water and as soon as the egg thickens add a teaspoon of lemon juice. Spread on slices of toasted brown bread and garnish with celery tips. Celery salt is a good addition to the seasoning.

RECHAUFFEE OF FINNAN HADDIE—Cover a finnan haddie with boiling water and let it simmer for twenty minutes, then remove the kettle and flake, discarding the skin and bones. For three cups of fish scald two cups of thin cream and add to the fish. Season with paprika or a dash of cayenne, and when thoroughly heated stir in the yolks of two eggs, diluted with a little hot cream.

SCALLOPED CLAMS IN SHELL—Chop the clams very fine and season with salt and cayenne pepper. In another dish mix some powdered crackers, moistened first with warm milk, then with clam liquor, a beaten egg and some melted butter, the quantity varying with the amount of clams used; stir in the chopped clams. Wash clean as many shells as the mixture will fill, wipe and butter them, fill heaping full with the mixture, smoothing with a spoon. Place in rows in a baking pan and bake until well browned. Send to the table hot.

SCALLOPED SHRIMPS—Make a sauce with a level tablespoon of cornstarch, a rounding tablespoon of butter and one cup of milk cooked together five minutes. Season with one-quarter level teaspoon of salt and a few grains of cayenne. Add one can of shrimps after removing all bits of shell and mincing them fine. Use, if preferred, the same amount of fresh shrimps. Put into buttered scallop shells, scatter fine bread crumbs over

ENTERPRISE

Meat Juice Extractor

☞ TINNED ☜

No. 21, $2.50
Directions sent with each machine

There is no one thing which, in cases of protracted illness or in imperfect nutrition, has to be served more often than beef juice. Beef juice is not beef tea, for the latter is weakened by the admixture of water, while the former is the pure and simple juice of the beef—nourishment in one of its most concentrated forms. In many homes, when sickness comes, much material and time are wasted by the primitive methods of extracting the beef juice needed. In such cases the possession of a **Meat Juice Extractor** is an economy, even could it be used for the meat alone. It can be used, however, in extracting fruit juices in small quantities, sufficient for invalid and convalescent dishes.

ACCORDING TO THIS AD IN *The Enterprising Housekeeper* (AN ADVERTISING COOKBOOK) THE TOP OF THE LINE MEAT JUICE EXTRACTOR COST ONLY $2.50 IN 1906. THE BOOK WAS WRITTEN BY HELEN LOUISE JOHNSON, AND OPENS WITH THIS POEM:
"We may live without poetry, music and art,
We may live without conscience and live without heart,
We may live without friends, we may live without books,
But civilized man cannot live without cooks."

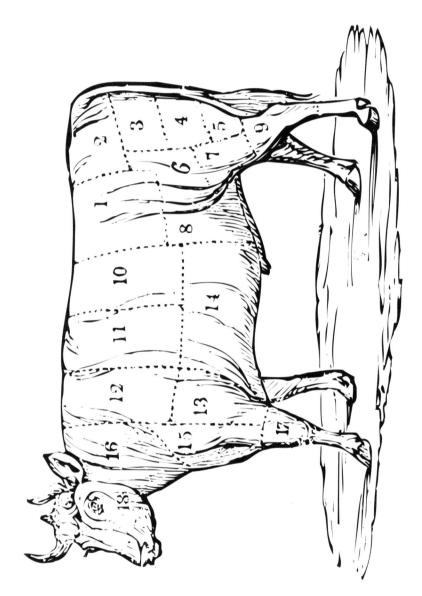

THIS BEEF CHART MAY HAVE BEEN USED BY BUTCHERS OF THE LATE 1800's.

Illustrator unknown.

the top of each, and dot with bits of butter. Set in a quick oven to brown the crumbs, and serve hot in the shells.

STEWED CODFISH—Take a piece of boiled cod, remove the skin and bones and pick into flakes. Put these in a stew-pan, with a little butter, salt, pepper, minced parsley and juice of a lemon. Put on the fire and when the contents of the pan are quite hot the fish is ready to serve.

CODFISH CONES—When it is not convenient to make and preparation into shapes, dip them into egg beaten with cream, then in sifted bread-crumbs and let them stand for half an hour or so to dry; then fry them a delicate color after plunging into boiling lard. Take them out, drain, place on a napkin on a dish and serve. The remainder of the chicken stock may be used for making consomme or soup.

BEEF, VEAL AND PORK

BEEF EN CASSEROLE—Have a steak cut two inches thick and broil two minutes on each side. Lay in a casserole and pour round two cups of rich brown sauce; add three onions cut in halves.

BEEF HASH CAKES—Chop cold corned beef fine and add a little more than the same measure of cold boiled potatoes, chopped less fine than the beef. Season with onion juice, make into small cakes, and brown in butter or beef drippings; serve each cake on a slice of buttered toast moistened slightly.

BEEF RAGOUT—Another way to serve the remnants of cold meat is to melt one rounding tablespoon of butter in a pan and let it brown lightly. Add two rounding tablespoons of flour and stir until smooth and browned; add one cup of strained tomato and one cup of stock or strained gravy, or part gravy and part water. When this sauce is thickened add two cups of meat cut in small, thin slices or shavings. Stir until heated through and no longer, as that will harden the meat. Season with salt and pepper, and serve at once.

BOILED BONED HAM—Wash a ham, place it in a sauce-pan, cover with cold water and boil for four or five hours, according to its size. Take out the bone, roll the ham and place it in a basin with a large weight on top. When cold put it on a dish, garnish with parsley, and serve.

BONED HAM—Have the bone taken from a small ham and put into a kettle of cold water with one onion cut in quarters, a dozen cloves, and a bay leaf. Cook slowly until tender and do not test it until you have allowed fifteen minutes to the pound. Take from the kettle, remove the skin, brush with beaten egg, sprinkle with bread crumbs and set in the oven to brown.

BREADED CUTLETS—Have the cutlets cut into portions of the right size for serving. Dust each side with salt and pepper. Beat one egg with a tablespoon of cold water, dip the cutlets in this and roll in fine bread crumbs. Fry three slices of salt pork in the frying-pan and cook the cutlets in this fat. As veal must be well done to be wholesome, cook it slowly about fifteen minutes. Serve with a gravy made from the contents of the pan or with a tomato sauce.

BROILED LIVER AND BACON—As broiling in most cases is wasteful, the liver and bacon are generally fried together, but the dish is somewhat spoiled by this method. The best way is to fry the well-trimmed slices of bacon, and after having washed and sliced the liver, say a third of an inch thick, dry it on a cloth and dip in flour. Place in the bacon fat and broil over a clear fire, adding pepper and salt while cooking. When done lay on a dish, placing a piece of bacon on each piece of liver.

BROILED PIG'S FEET—Thoroughly clean as many pig's feet as are required, and split lengthwise in halves, tying them with a broad tape so they will not open in cooking. Put in a saucepan with a seasoning of parsley, thyme, bayleaf, allspice, carrots and onions, with sufficient water to cover. Boil slowly until tender, and let them cool in the liquor. Dip in the beaten yolks of eggs and warmed butter. Sprinkle with salt and pepper and cover with bread crumbs seasoned with very finely chopped shallot and parsley. Put on a gridiron over a clear fire and broil until well and evenly browned. Unbind and arrange on a dish, garnish with fried parsley and serve.

BROILED SHEEP'S KIDNEYS—To broil sheep's kidneys cut them open, put them on small skewers. Season with salt and pepper and broil. When done serve with shallot or maitre d'hotel sauce.

BRUNSWICK STEW—Cut up one chicken, preferably a good fat hen, cover with cold water, season with salt and pepper, and cook slowly until about half done. Add six ears of green corn, splitting through the kernels, one pint butter beans and six large tomatoes chopped fine. A little onion may be added if desired. Cook until the vegetables are thoroughly done, but very slowly, so as to avoid burning. Add strips of pastry for dumplings and cook five minutes. Fresh pork can be used in place of the chicken and canned vegetables instead of the fresh.

CALVES' TONGUES—Wash and put into a saucepan with half a dozen slices of carrot an onion sliced, five cloves, a teaspoon of whole peppercorns, and half a level tablespoon of salt. Cover with boiling water and simmer until tender. Drain and cool a little, then take off the skin. Drop back into the hot liquid to reheat. Serve with a sauce. Melt one-quarter cup of butter, add three slightly rounding tablespoons of flour, stir and cook until browned, add two cups of broth, brown stock of rich gravy melted in hot water, one-half level teaspoon of salt, the same of paprika, a saltspoon of allspice, one tablespoon of vinegar, a few grains of cayenne, and half a tablespoon of capers. Pour over the tongues and serve.

CORNED BEEF HASH—To two cups of chopped cold corned beef, add two cups of chopped cold boiled potatoes. Heat three tablespoons of bacon fat in a frying pan and add the meat and potato, add pepper and salt, if necessary, and moisten with water. Cook slowly until a nice brown underneath. Roll from the pan on to a hot platter. Garnish with parsley and serve with pickled beets.

ENGLISH POT ROAST—Cut one pound of cold roast into two-inch pieces, slice four good sized potatoes thin, also one onion, into a deep dish, put a layer of the beef, one of potatoes, one of onions, salt and pepper, another layer of meat, potatoes and onions, season again, add one cup gravy, and over all put a thick layer of potatoes. Bake three hours—the longer and slower the better.

FRANKFORT SAUSAGE—For this use any part of the pig, but equal quantities of lean and fat. Mince fine, season with ground coriander seed, salt, pepper, and a small quantity of nut-meg. Have ready skins, well cleaned and soaked in cold water for several hours, fill with the seasoned meat, secure the ends and hang in a cool, dry place until needed.

FRIED HAM—Cut off a thick slice of ham. Place in a saucepan over the fire, with sufficient water to cover and let come to a boil. Pour off the water, and fry the ham slowly until it is brown on both sides. Season with pepper and serve. Eggs are usually served with fried ham. They may be fried in the same pan or separately, in sufficient grease to prevent burning. Season with salt and pepper, place around the ham.

HAM AND CHICKEN PIE—Trim off the skin of some cold chicken and cut the meat into small pieces. Mix with an equal quantity of finely chopped lean ham and a small lot of chopped shallot. Season with salt, pepper and pounded mace, moisten with a few tablespoonfuls of white stock. Butter a pie dish, line the edges with puff paste and put in the mixture, placing puff paste over the top. Trim it around the edges, moisten and press together, cut a small hole in the top, and bake in a moderate oven. When cooked, pour a small quantity of hot cream through the hole in the top of the pie, and serve.

HAM CROQUETTES—Chop very fine one-fourth of a pound of ham; mix with it an equal quantity of boiled and mashed potatoes, two hard boiled eggs chopped, one tablespoonful chopped parsley. Season to taste. Then stir in the yolk of an egg. Flour the hands and shape the mixture into small balls. Fry in deep fat. Place on a dish, garnish with parsley and serve.

HASH WITH DROPPED EGGS—Mince or grind cold cooked meat and add two-thirds as much cold chopped vegetables. The best proportions of vegetables are half potato and one-quarter each of beets and carrots. Put a little gravy stock or hot water with butter melted in it, into a saucepan, turn in the meat and vegetables and heat, stirring all the time. Season with salt, pepper, and a little onion juice if liked. Turn into a buttered baking dish, smooth over, and set in the oven to brown. Take up and press little depressions in the top, and drop an egg into each. Set back into the oven until the egg is set, but not cooked hard. Serve in the same dish.

LAMB CHOPS EN CASSEROLE—Trim off the superfluous fat from the chops, and place them in a casserole with a medium sized onion, sliced and separated into rings. Cover each layer of chops with the onion rings, then add a pint of boiling water. Cover and cook for one hour and one-half in a moderate oven. Add salt and pepper and some sliced carrot, and cook until the carrot is tender. Remove the chops to a hot platter and pour over them the gravy which may be thickened, then garnish with the carrot.

LAMB CURRY—Cut the meat into small pieces, (and the inferior portions, such as the neck can be utilized in a curry), roll in flour and fry in hot olive oil, pork fat, or butter, until a rich brown. Mince or slice an onion and fry in the same way. Then put into a saucepan, cover with boiling water, and simmer until the bones and gristly pieces will slip out. When the meat is sufficiently tender add a cupful each strained tomato and rice, then a powder. Cook ten minutes longer and serve.

MEAT PIE—Chop fine, enough of cold roast beef to make two cupfuls, also one small onion, pare as many potatoes as desired and boil, mash and cream as for mashed potatoes. Drain a cupful of tomato liquid free from seeds, stir meat, onion and tomato juice together, put in a deep dish, spread potatoes over the top and bake in a hot oven.

MINCED MUTTON—Mince the meat from a cold roast of mutton, put into a sacepan. Make a rous, moisten with a little stock and season with salt and pepper, adding butter and some gherkins. Put the minced meat into the sauce and let it cook without boiling. Serve with thin slices of bread around the plate.

PIG'S EARS, LYONAISE—Singe off all the hair from pig's ears, scrape and wash well and cut lengthwise into strips. Place them in a saucepan with a little stock, add a small quantity of flour, a few slices of onion fried, salt and pepper to taste. Place the pan over a slow fire and simmer until the ears are thoroughly cooked. Arrange on a dish, add a little lemon juice to the liquor and pour over the ears. Serve with a garnish of fried bread.

PORK CUTLETS AND ANCHOVY SAUCE—Broil on a well greased gridiron, over the fire, nicely cut and trimmed cut-lets of pork. Place frills on the bones of the cutlets. Serve very hot with Anchovy Sauce.

RAGOUT OF COOKED MEAT—Cut one pint of cold meat into half-inch dice, removing the fat, bone and gristle. Put the meat into a stew pan, cover with boiling water and simmer slowly two or three hours or until very tender. Then add half a can of mushrooms cut fine, two tablespoons of lemon juice and salt and pepper to taste. Wet one tablespoonful of cornstarch to a smooth paste with a little cold water and stir into the boiling liquor, add a teaspoon of caramel if not brown enough. Cook ten minutes and serve plain or in a border of mashed potatoes. The seasoning may be varied by using one teaspoon of curry powder, a few grains of cayenne or half a tumbler of currant jelly and salt to taste.

RICE AND BEEF CROQUETTES—To use up cold meat economically combine two cups of chopped beef or mutton with two cups of freshly boiled rice. Season well with salt, pepper, onion juice, a large teaspoon of minced parsley, and a teaspoon of lemon juice. Pack on a large plate and set away to cool. After the mixture is cold, shape into croquettes, dip into beaten egg, roll in fine crumbs and fry in smoking hot fat.

ROLLED RIB ROAST—Have the backbone and ribs removed and utilize them for making a stew for lunch. Tie the meat into a round shape and sprinkle it with salt and pepper, then dredge with flour and place in a dripping pan. Have the oven hot when the meat is first put into it, in order that it may be seared over quickly to prevent the juices from escaping. Then reduce the heat and baste with the fat in the pan. When done place on a hot platter and surround with riced potato.

SHEEP'S BRAINS, WITH SMALL ONIONS—Take sheep's brains. Soak in lukewarm water and blanch. Stew with thin slices of bacon, a little white wine, parsley, shallots, cloves, small onions, salt and pepper. When done arrange the brains on a dish, with the onions around; reduce the cause and serve. Calves' brains may be dressed in the same way.

SHEEP'S TONGUES—Sheep's tongues are usually boiled in water and then broiled. To dress them, first skin and split down the center. Dip them in butter or sweet oil, mixed with parsley, green onions, mushrooms, clove of garlic, all shredded fine, salt and pepper. Then cover with bread crumbs and broil. Serve with an acid sauce.

SHOULDER OF VEAL BRAISED—Buy a shoulder of veal and ask the butcher to bone it and send the bones with the meat. Cover the bones with cold water and when it comes to a boil skim, then add a little onion and carrot and a few seasoning herbs and any spices desired. Simmer gently for an hour or so until you have a pint of stock. To make the stuffing take a stale loaf, cut off the crust and soak in a little cold water until soft. Rub the crumbs of the loaf as fine as possible in the hands, then add to the soaked and softened crust. Chop a half cup of suet fine, put into a frying pan a tablespoon of the suet, and when hot add an onion chopped fine. Cook until brown then add to the bread with regular poultry seasoning or else salt, pepper, and a bit of thyme. Mix well and stuff the cavity in the shoulder, then pull the flaps of the meat over and sew up. Put the rest of the suet in the frying pan and having dusted the meat with flour, salt and pepper and a sprinking of sugar, brown on all sides in the fat into the bottom of the braising pan, which may be any shallow iron pot or granite kettle with a tight cover, put a layer of thin sliced onions and carrots, a bit of bay leaf and sprigs of parsley, and on this lay the meat. Add two or three cloves, pour hot stock around it, cover closely and braise in a hot oven for three hours.

SPANISH CHOPS—Gash six French chops on outer edge, extending cut more than half way through lean meat. Stuff, dip in crumbs, egg and crumbs, fry in deep fat five minutes and drain on brown paper.

For the stuffing mix six tablespoons of soft bread crumbs, three tablespoons of chopped cooked ham, two tablespoons chopped mushroom caps, two tablespoons melted butter, salt and pepper to taste.

HARICOT OF MUTTON—To make a la bourgeiose, cut a shoulder of mutton in pieces about the width of two fingers. Mix a little butter with a tablespoonful of flour and place over a slow fire, stirring until the color of cinnamon. Put in the pieces of meat, giving them two or three turns over the fire, then add some stock, if you have it, or about half pint of hot water, which must be stirred in a little at a time. Season with salt, pepper, parsley, green onions, bay leaf, thyme, garlic, cloves, and basil. Set the whole over a slow fire and when half done skim off as much fat as possible. Have ready some turnips, cut in pieces, and stew with the meat. When done take out the herbs and skim off what fat remains, reducing the stock if too thin.

VEAL CROQUETTES—Make a thick sauce from one cup of milk, two level tablespoons of butter, and four level table-spoons of flour. Cook five minutes, season with salt, pepper and celery salt, and a few drops of lemon juice, and a tablespoon of finely minced parsley. Add two cups of cold cooked veal chopped fine and cool the mixture. Shape into little rolls, dip in an egg beaten with one tablespoon of water then roll in fine bread crumbs. Fry in deep smoking hot fat. Be sure to coat the whole surface with egg and to have the fat very hot, as the mixture has been cooked once and merely needs beating to the center and browning on the outside.

VEAL LOAF—Mince fine three pounds lean raw veal and a quarter of a pound of fat pork. Add a half onion chopped fine or grated, a tablespoonful of salt, a teaspoonful pepper and a teaspoonful seasoning herbs. Mix well, add two-thirds of a cup cracker crumbs, a half cup veal gravy, the yolk of one egg and the whites of two beaten together. Form into a loaf, pressing firmly together. Brush over with the yolk of an egg, dust with finely rolled cracker crumbs and set in a greased rack in the dripping pan. When it begins to brown, turn a cup of hot water into the pan and baste frequently until done. It will take about an hour and a half in a moderate oven.

VEAL PATTIES—Make a sauce of two level tablespoons each of butter and flour, one cup of stock or boiling water, and one cup of thin cream. Cook five minutes, add two cups of finely chopped cooked veal, half a level teaspoon of salt, a saltspoon of pepper, also the beaten yolks of two eggs, and a tablespoon of finely minced parsley. As soon as the egg thickens take from the fire and fill hot pastry cases.

VIRGINIA STEW—A half grown chicken or two squirrels, one slice of salt pork, twelve large tomatoes, three cups of lima beans, one large onion, two large Irish potatoes, twelve ears of corn, one-fourth pound of butter, one-fourth pound of lard, one gallon of boiling water, two tablespoonfuls salt and pepper; mix as any ordinary soup and let it cook for a couple of hours of more, then serve.

BROILING STEAK—While many prefer steak fairly well done, still the great majority desire to have it either rare, or certainly not overdone. For those who wish a steak well done—completely though—and still not to have the outside crisp to a cinder, it is necessary to cut the steak possibly as thin as one-half inch, and then the outside can have that delicious and intense scorching which quickly prevents the escape of juices, and also gives the slightly burned taste which at its perfect condition is the most delicious flavor from my own preference that can be given to a steak. By this I do not mean a steak burned to a cinder, but slightly scorched over a very hot fire.

FOR RARE BROILED STEAK—For those who are fond of rare steak it can be cut from one inch to one and one-quarter inches in thickness and the outside thoroughly and quickly broiled, leaving the inside practically only partially cooked, so that the blood will follow the knife and still the steak has been heated completely through and a thin crust on either side has been well cooked, which has formed the shell to retain the juices.

PROPERLY FRYING STEAK—To fry steak properly (although some claim it is not proper to fry steak under any circumstances), it is necessary to have the butter, oleo, fat or grease piping hot, for two reasons: First, the steak sears over quickly, and the juices are thus retained within the steak to bet-ter advantage than by the slow process of cooking, but even more important is the fact that the incrustation thus formed not only holds the juices within the steak, but prevents the fat from penetrating and making the steak greasy, soggy and unat-tractive. As a rule, however, we must acknowledge that broiled steak is in varying degrees largely superior to fried steak.

BROILED LOIN STEAKS—Two loin steaks of about a pound each: season with salt and pepper to taste, baste on either side with a little oil. Place on a broiler over a bright charcoal fire, and broil for six minutes, on each side. Serve on a hot dish with Bordeaux sauce and garnish with rounds of marrow.

FRIED HAMBURG STEAK, WITH RUSSIAN SAUCE— Select a piece of buttock beef, remove the fat and chop very fine. Add finely chopped shallot, two eggs, salt, pepper, and grated nutmeg. Mix well and form into balls. Roll in bread crumbs and fry with a little clarified butter four or five minutes, turning frequently. Serve with Russian sauce.

FRIED SAUSAGE MEAT—Roll sausage meat into small balls, wrapping each in a thin rasher of bacon and fasten with a skewer. Fry lightly in a little butter. Serve with fried parsley and crutons of fried bread. Serve hot.

ROAST BEEF, AMERICAN STYLE—Lay the meat on sticks in a dripping pan, so as not to touch the water which is placed in the bottom of the pan. Season with salt and pepper and roast for three or four hours, basting frequently. When done sift over the top browned cracker crumbs and garnish with parsley.

ROAST BEEF ON SPIT—Remove most of the flap from sir-loin and trim neatly. Have a clear brisk fire and place the meat close to it for the first half hour, then move it farther away, bast-ing frequently, and when done sprinkle well with salt. The gravy may be prepared by taking the meat from the dripping pan which will have a brown sediment. Pour in some boiling water and salt. Strain over the meat. A thickening of flour may be added if necessary. Garnish with horseradish and serve with horseradish sauce.

ROAST RIBS OF BEEF—Break off the ends of the bones of the desired amount of ribs; take out the shin-bone, and place the meat in a baking pan. Sprinkle with salt and spread some small lumps of butter over it and dust with flour, baking in a moderate oven till done. Serve hot and garnish with horse-radish.

ROAST SHOULDER OF PORK—Remove the bone from a shoulder of pork and spread it over inside with a stuffing of sage and onions, filling the cavity where the bone was taken out. Roll up and secure with a string, put in a pan and roast in a very hot oven till done. When done put on a dish, skim off the fat in the pan, add a little water and a tablespoon of made mustard, boil the gravy once and pass through a strainer over the meat and serve.

SMOKED BEEF WITH CREAM—Place the finely minced beef in a stew-pan with a lump of butter, cooking it for two minutes, and moisten slightly with a little cream, add two tablespoonfuls of bechamel sauce. Serve as soon as it boils up.

STEAK—Cut the steak half an inch thick from between the two ribs, remove all gristle and fat, and trim in the shape of a flat pear. Sprinkle both sides with salt, pepper and oil to prevent outside hardening. Broil ten minutes over a moderate and even fire. Place about four ounces of maitre d'hotel butter on a dish. Lay the steak upon it and garnish with fried potatoes, serving either piquant, D'Italian, or tomato sauce.

STEWED SAUSAGE WITH CABBAGE—Procure a medium sized white cabbage, remove all the green leaves, and cut it into quarters, removing the center stalks. Wash thoroughly in cold water, drain well and cut into small pieces. Put in boiling salted water for five minutes. Take out and put in cold water and cool moderately. Drain in a colander and put in a saucepan with one gill of fat from soup stock or one ounce of butter. Season with a pinch of salt and one-half pinch of pepper, a medium sized onion and a carrot cut into small quarters. Put on the cover of the saucepan, set on a moderate fire and cook for half an hour. Take twelve sausages, prick them with a fork, add them to the cabbage and allow all to cook together for twelve minutes. Dress the cabbage on a hot dish and arrange the sau-sages and carrot on top. Serve very hot.

SUCKLING PIG—The pig should not be more than a month or six weeks old, and if possible should be dressed the day after it is killed. First, scald it as follows: Soak the pig in cold water for fifteen minutes, then plunge it into boiling water. Hold it by the head and shake around until the hairs begin to loosen.

VOLUME XV.   NEW YORK, MARCH 27, 1890.   NUMBER 378.

Entered at the New York Post Office as Second-Class Mail Matter.
Copyright, 1890, by MITCHELL & MILLER.

OF SAD EXPERIENCE.

"PAPA, WHAT IS A GREEN-GROCER?"
"HE'S A GROCER WHO TRIES TO SELL SUGAR WITHOUT SAND IN IT."

COVER FROM *Life* MAGAZINE, MARCH 27, 1890,
POKES FUN AT THE DIFFERENCE BETWEEN A GROCER
WHO SELLS "GREEN" OR FRESH VEGETABLES,
AND A GROCER TOO "GREEN" OR NEW AT HIS TRADE TO
TAKE ADVANTAGE OF CUSTOMERS.

THE CAPTION READS:
"Papa, what is a green-grocer?"
"He's a grocer who tries to sell sugar without sand in it."

" ... PETER'S PA, TO SAY NOTHING OF HIS MA, HAD BROUGHT UP
THEIR CHILDREN TO BE VERY PARTICULAR IN THE OBSERVANCE
OF TABLE MANNERS."

Illustration by Louise A. Field from the children's book Peter Rabbit and His Pa, *written by Virginia Albert, and published by the Saalfield Publishing Company in 1916.*

Take out of the water and rub vigorously with a coarse towel, until all hairs are removed. Cut the pig open, remove the entrails, wash thoroughly in cold water. Dry on a towel, cut the feet off at the first joint leaving enough skin to turn over and keep it wrapped in a wet cloth until ready for use.

SALADS

ASPARAGUS SALAD—Cook the asparagus in salted water, drain and chill. Serve with French dressing or sprinkle lightly with a little oil dressing; let stand a half hour and serve with mayonnaise or boiled dressing, as any one of the three distinct kinds is appropriate with this salad.

BEET SALAD—Bake the beets until tender, remove the skins and place them in the ice box to chill. Shred a white cabbage finely and sprinkle well with salt and use lettuce leaves to line the salad bowl. Slice the beets, place them on the lettuce, spread with a layer of cabbage, garnish with sliced beets cut in points and dress with mayonnaise or boiled dressing.

BIRDS NEST SALAD—Have ready as many crisp leaves of lettuce as may be required to make a dainty little nest for each person. Curl them into shape and in each one place tiny speckled eggs made by rolling cream cheese into shape, then sprinkle with fine chopped parsley. Serve with French dressing hidden under the leaves of the nest.

CABBAGE SALAD—Chop or shave fine, half a medium size head of cabbage that has been left in cold water until crisp, then drain. Season with salt and pepper, then pour over it a dressing made this way: Beat the yolks of two eggs, add two tablespoons of melted butter and beat again. Add two tablespoons thick sour cream, two tablespoons sugar, a sprinkle of mustard and half cup of vinegar. Beat until thoroughly mixed, pour over the cabbage and toss lightly until uniformly seasoned.

CAULIFLOWER MAYONNAISE—Take cold boiled cauliflower, break into branches, adding salt, pepper and vinegar to season. Heap on a platter, making the flowers come to a point at the top. Surround with a garnish of cooked and diced carrots, turnips, green peas. Pour mayonnaise over all, chill and serve. Another garnish for cauliflower is pickled beets.

CELERY AND NUT SALAD—Cut enough celery fine to measure two cups, add one cup of finely shredded or shaved cabbage and one and one-half cups of walnut meats, broken in small pieces, but not chopped. Mix and moisten on a serving dish and garnish with celery tips.

CREOLE SALAD—Half cup of olive oil, five tablespoons of vinegar, half teaspoon of powdered sugar, one teaspoon salt, two tablespoons chopped red pepper, three tablespoons chopped green peppers, half Bermuda onion, parsley and lettuce and serve.

FISH SALAD—Remove skin and bones and flake cold cooked fish. Sprinkle with salt and pepper and add a few drops of lemon juice. Arrange on a bed of shredded lettuce in the shape of a fish. Cover with mayonnaise or cream dressing and garnish with hard boiled eggs and parsley.

JELLIED CUCUMBER—Pare and slice cucumbers and cook in water to cover until tender. Drain, season with salt, a few grains of cayenne, and to one cup of the cooked cucumber add a level teaspoon of gelatin dissolved in a spoonful of cold water. Stir the soaked gelatin in while the cucumber is hot. Set into a cold place to chill and become firm. If a large mold is used break up roughly into pieces, if small molds are taken then unmold onto lettuce leaves and serve with mayonnaise.

NUT AND CELERY SALAD—Cover one cup of walnut meats and two slices of onion with boiling water, to which is added a teaspoon of salt. Cook half an hour, drain, turn into ice cold water for ten minutes, then rub off the brown skin. Add the nuts broken in small pieces to two cups of celery cut in small pieces crosswise. Use only the white inner stalks, serve with a cream dressing.

SALAD—Two cups of apples cut into small pieces, one cup celery cut into small pieces, one cup English walnuts. Serve on a lettuce leaf with mayonnaise dressing, made without mustard, and thinned with cream. Garnish dish that dressing is made in with a little garlic.

SPANISH TOMATOES—Choose ten or a dozen large tomatoes, cut a slice from the stem end of each and scoop out the inside. Put the pulp into a basin with two ounces of melted butter, two tablespoonfuls of lemon juice, half a pound of chestnuts, boiled and grated, and seasoning of salt and white pepper to taste. Fill the tomatoes with this, which should be about the consistency of thick cream, spread with a thick mayonnaise, garnish with chopped parsley and serve on lettuce leaves.

TOMATO BASKETS—Tomato baskets are charming accessories for holding vegetable salad, chicken, shrimps, cold beans, asparagas tips, shredded celery, cucumbers cut in cubes and minced peppers. Choose firm, smooth tomatoes, not too large and as nearly one size as possible. Dip for half a minute in boiling water, skin and set in ice box to chill. Cut out pulp and seeds, dress the cavity with salt, pepper, oil and vinegar, then fill with the salad, seasoned with French dressing or mayonnaise. Handles of watercress may be attached to these baskets. Set on lettuce or cress, as desired.

TRIANON SALAD—Cut one grape fruit and two oranges in sections and free from seeds and membrane. Skin and seed one cup white grapes and cut one-third cup pecan nut meats in small pieces. Mix ingredients, arrange on a bed of romaine and pour over the following dressing: Mix four tablespoons olive oil, one tablespoon grape juice, one tablespoon grape vinegar, one-fourth teaspoon paprika, one-eighth teaspoon pepper and one tablespoon finely chopped Roquefort cheese. This dressing should stand in the ice-box four or five hours to become seasoned.

CREAM DRESSING—Mix one-half level tablespoon each of salt and mustard, three-quarters level tablespoon of sugar, one egg slightly beaten, two and one-half tablespoons of melted butter, three-quarters cup of cream, and heat in a double boiler. When hot add very slowly one-quarter cup of hot vinegar, stirring all the time. When thickened strain and cool.

FRENCH DRESSING—For party of six five tablespoons of oil and three of vinegar, juice of half lemon, two drops tobasco, tablespoon of salt, slice of onion, and boil for three minutes and ready for service. Strain and bottle and put in ice box, shake before using each time.

SALAD DRESSING—When making salad for a large family take quart bottle with a rather wide mouth, put in one-half cup of vinegar, one and one-half cups of olive oil, two level teaspoons of salt and one-half level teaspoon of pepper; cork the bottle tightly and shake vigorously until an emulsion is made. The proportion of vinegar may be larger if not very strong and more salt and pepper used if liked. Use from the bottle and shake well each time any is used.

Instructions for Preparing Poultry Before Dressing.

To serve poultry tender and delicate, it should be kept some hours after being killed before boiling or roasting. Poultry intended for dinner should be killed the evening before. When poultry has ceased to bleed, before picking put it into cold water, in a vessel large enough to completely cover it. Then take out and soak in boiling water for a few minutes. Pick it, being careful to take out all the small feathers. When cleaning the inside of poultry or game be sure not to break the gall bladder, for it will give a bitter taste to the meat. Be equally careful not to tear the intestines near the gizzard, as it will make the inside dirty and spoil the whole bird.

They're Laying For The Man.
Who Feeds Them
Watkins Poultry Tonic

HEALTHY, thrifty, poultry and an abundance of eggs are sure to be the result where Watkins Poultry Tonic is used. If you want your chickens to do the right thing by you, you must do the right thing by them. Keep them growing strong and vigorous by mixing a small daily ration of Watkins Poultry Tonic with their regular feed. It has no equal as an egg producer and growth promotor. Watkins Poultry Tonic makes fowls pay. It makes hens lay. The annual egg crop amounts to as much as the wheat crop It is far more profitable. Watkins Poultry Tonic increases the yield of eggs and multiplies the profits. It contains just the food qualities that fowls need for quick growth or egg production. It is a tonic, a stimulant, a regulator and a germicide with purifying qualities that make it a preventative of disease. Cholera, Roup and other destructive diseases are not found among flocks whose feed contains Watkins Poultry Tonic and whose quarters are sprayed with Watkins Stock Dip.

Watkins Poultry Tonic insures better digestion and a greater amount of nourishment on less feed and at slight expense. Treat your hens to regular feeds of Watkins Poultry Tonic and they will treat you generously to fresh eggs when fresh eggs are rare and high priced. A FEW dozen eggs will pay for a pail of Watkins Poultry Tonic.

One Pail of Watkins Poultry Tonic
Will Produce Many Dozen Eggs

ADVERTISEMENT FOR WATKINS POULTRY TONIC
FROM THE 1913 *Watkins Almanac.*

Published by the *J. R. Watkins Medical Company of Winona, Minnesota.*

THE LITTLE RED HEN SAID,
"WHO WILL HELP ME PLANT THE WHEAT?"

"NOT I," SAID THE CAT.

"NOT I," SAID THE GOOSE.

"NOT I," SAID THE PIG.

"THEN I WILL PLANT THE WHEAT," SAID THE LITTLE RED HEN.

AND SHE DID.

The Winston Readers Primer,
by Sidney G. Firman and Ethel H. Maltby.
Illustrated by Frederick Richardson in 1918.

POULTRY AND POULTRY DRESSINGS

BOHEMIAN CHICKEN—Select a young and tender chicken and prepare as for frying or broiling. Place in a frying pan a pat of butter and place on the fire. Beat to a smooth, thin batter two eggs, three spoonfuls of milk and a little flour, season, dip each piece of the chicken in this batter and fry a rich brown in the heated butter.

CHICKEN A LA TARTARE—Have a chicken dressed and split down the back; it should not weigh over two and a half pounds. Put one quarter cup of butter in a frying pan with a teaspoon of finely minced parsley, half a teaspoon of salt and a little pepper. Brown each half of the chicken in the butter and on both sides. Take up the chicken, brush the inside over with an egg beaten with one tablespoon of cold water, lay in a dripping pan and dust over the egg half a cup of fine bread crumbs mixed with the same amount of minced cooked ham. Set in a hot oven and finish cooking. Serve on a hot dish with sauce tartare. The chicken will cook best if laid in a wire broiler resting on the dripping pan.

CHICKEN BROILED IN PAPER—Split a chicken and let it soak for two hours in oil mixed with parsley, sliced onion, cloves, salt and pepper. Put each half in papers, enclosing all the seasoning and broil over a very slow fire. When done take off the paper, bacon, etc., and serve with sauce a la ravigotte.

CHICKEN CROQUETTES—Stir a pint of fine chopped chicken into a cup and a quarter of sauce made of one-third cup of flour, three tablespoons of butter, a cup of chicken stock and one-fourth cup of cream, season with a few drops of onion juice, a teaspoon of lemon, one teaspoonful celery salt and pepper. When thoroughly chilled form into cylindrical shapes, roll in egg and bread crumbs and fry in deep fat. Serve surrounded with peas and figures stamped upon cooked slices of carrot. Season with salt, paprika and butter.

CHICKEN CROQUETTE—Take two chickens weighing about two pounds each, put them into a saucepan with water to cover, add two onions and carrots, a small bunch of parsley and thyme, a few cloves and half a grated nutmeg, and boil until birds are tender; then remove the skin, gristle and sinews and chop the meat as fine as possible. Put into a saucepan one pound of butter and two tablespoonfuls of flour, stir over the fire for a few minutes and add half a pint of the liquor the chickens were cooked in and one pint of rich cream, and boil for eight or ten minutes, stirring continually. Remove the pan from the fire, season with salt, pepper, grated nutmeg and a little powdered sweet marjoram, add the chopped meat and stir well. Then stir in rapidly the yolks of four eggs, place the saucepan on the fire for a minute, stirring well, turn the mass onto a dish, spread it out and let it get cold. Cover the hands with flour and form the preparation into shapes, dip them into egg beaten with cream, then in sifted breadcrumbs and let them stand for half an hour or so to dry; then fry them a delicate color after plunging into boiling lard. Take them out, drain, place on a napkin on a dish and serve. The remainder of the chicken stock may be used for making consomme or soup.

CHICKEN CROQUETTES WITH FISH FLAVOR—The foundation of all croquettes is a thick white sauce which stiffens when cold, so that mixed with minced fish, chicken or other compounds it can be easily handled and shaped into pears, cylinders, ovals, etc. When cooked the croquettes should be soft and creamy inside. This sauce is made as follows:—

Scald in a double boiler one pint rich milk or cream. Melt in a granite saucepan two even tablespoons butter, then add two heaping tablespoonfuls cornstarch or flour, and one tablespoon of flavor.

When blended add one-third of the hot cream and keep stirring as it cooks and thickens. When perfectly smooth put in all the cream. The sauce should be very thick. Add the season-ing, a half teaspoonful of salt, a half teaspoonful celery salt, white peppers or paprika to taste, then the meat.

In shaping the croquettes take about a tablespoonful of the mixture and handling gently and carefully, press gently into whatever shape is desired. Have ready a board sprinkled lightly with bread or cracker crumbs, and roll the croquettes lightly in this, taking care not to exert pressure sufficient to break them. Coat the croquettes with some slightly salted beaten egg. Then roll again in the crumbs. Fry in deep hot fat, a few at a time, then drain on paper.

CHICKEN POT PIE—Cut a fowl into pieces to serve and cook in water to cover until the bones will come out easily. Be-fore taking them out drop dumplings in, cover closely and cook ten minutes without lifting the cover. The liquid should be boiling rapidly when the dough is put in and kept boiling until the end. For the dumplings sift two cups of flour twice with half a level teaspoon of salt and four level teaspoons of baking powder. Mix with about seven-eighths cup of milk, turn out on a well floured board and pat out half an inch thick. Cut into small cakes. If this soft dough is put into the kettle in spoonfuls the time of cooking must be doubled. The bones and meat will keep the dough from settling into the liq-uid and becoming soggy. Arrange the meat in the center, with dumplings around the edge and a sprig of parsley between each. Thicken the liquid and season with salt and pepper as needed and a rounding table-spoon of butter.

CHICKEN TIMBALES—Mix three-fourths of a cupful of flour with a half teaspoonful of salt. Add gradually while stir-ring constantly, one-half cupful of milk and one well beaten egg and one tablespoonful of olive oil. Shape, using a hot Swedish timbale iron, and cook in deep fat until delicately brown. Take from the iron and invert on brown paper to drain. To make the filling for a dozen timbales, remove bones and skin from a pint bowlful of the white or white and dark meat mixed of cold boiled or roasted chicken, and cut in half inch pieces. Put over the first in a saucepan two tablespoonfuls of butter and two of flour and when melted and blended add milk and chicken broth, a cupful and a half or more as desired to make a rich cream sauce. Season with salt and pepper, add the chicken and, if pre-ferred, one-half cupful of mushrooms cut in pieces the same size as the chicken. Then brown in butter before adding to the sauce. Fill the timbales.

DEVILED CHICKEN—Split the chickens down the back and broil until done, lay on a hot dripping pan and spread on a sauce, scatter fine crumbs over and set in a quick oven to brown. For the sauce beat a rounding tablespoon of butter light with one-half teaspoon of mixed mustard, one teaspoon of vinegar and a pinch of cayenne.

FRICASSED TURKEY OR GOOSE GIBLETS—Scald and pick giblets. Put them in a saucepan with a piece of butter, a bunch of parsley, green onions, thyme, bay-leaf and a few mushrooms; warm these over the fire, with a sprinkle of flour moistened with stock or water, adding salt and pepper to taste. Reduce to a thick sauce, adding to it the yolks of two eggs, and let simmer without boiling. Serve with sprinkling of vinegar.

FRIED CHICKEN—Cut up two chickens. Put a quarter of a pound of butter, mixed with a spoonful of flour, into a saucepan with pepper, salt, little vinegar, parsley, green onions, carrots and turnips, into a saucepan and heat. Steep the chicken in this marinade three hours, having dried the pieces and floured them. Fry a good brown. Garnish with fried parsley.

JELLIED CHICKEN—For jellied chicken have on hand three pounds of chicken that has been boiled and cut from the bone in strips. Mix a quart of rich chicken stock that has been boiled down and cleared with a teaspoonful each of lemon juice, chopped parsley, a dash of celery salt and a quarter teaspoonful each of salt and paprika. At the last stir in a teaspoonful of granulated gelatin that has been dissolved. When the jelly begins to thicken add the chicken and turn it into a mold. To have the chicken scattered evenly through the jelly, stand the dish containing the jelly in a pan of ice and turn in the jelly layer by layer, covering each with chicken a soon as it begins to thicken.

MARBLED CHICKEN—Steam a young fowl until tender or cook it gently in a small amount of water. Cut all the meat from the bones, keeping the white and dark meat separate. Chop the meat with a sharp knife, but do not grind it, season with salt and pepper. Press into a mold making alternate layers of light and dark meat. Strain the broth in which the fowl was cooked and which should be reduced by cooking to a small amount, season with salt and pepper, add a tablespoon of butter after skimming clear of all fat. Pour this broth over the meat and set all in the ice chest until cold and firm. Unmold and cut in thin slices with a sharp knife, then if liked garnish with cress and sliced lemon and serve.

POTTED CHICKEN—Truss a small broiler in shape and lay in casserole. Brush it generously with melted butter, put on the cover, and cook twenty minutes. Now add one cup of rich stock or beef extract dissolved in hot water to make a good strength. Cover and finish cooking. Serve uncovered in the same dish with spoonfuls of potato balls, small carrots sliced and tiny string beans laid alternately round the chicken. The vege-tables should each be cooked separately.

PRESSED CHICKEN—Cut as for a stew. Skin the feet and place in the bottom of a stew pan. Arrange the fowl on top, just cover with water, and cook slowly until tender. Do not let the meat brown. Separate the dark and light meat and throw away the feet, from which the gluten has been extracted. Chop liver, skin, heart and gizzard fine. Add these chopped giblets to a dressing of stale bread crumbs seasoned and moistened with a little hot water and butter. Arrange the large pieces of meat around the sides and bottom of a baking dish, alternating dark and light, and fill alternately with dressing and chicken until the dish is full. Remove the fat from the water in which the chicken was cooked, heat boiling hot and pour over the chicken. Put into a press for several hours and when cold slice.

ROAST CHICKEN—Having drawn and brussed the chicken put it between some slices of bacon, take care to fasten the feet to the spit to keep it together, baste it with its gravy, when well done through, serve with cress round the dish, season with salt and vinegar. The chicken and bacon should be covered with buttered paper, until five minutes of the bird being done, then take off the paper, and finish the roasting by a very bright fire.

STUFFED CHICKEN—Put a pint of milk into a saucepan with a good handful of crumbs of bread and boil until very thick. Set away to cool. Add to this parsley, chopped green onion, thyme, salt, pepper, piece of butter and the yolks of four eggs, and place in doby of chicken, sewing up the opening. Roast the chicken between rashers of bacon.

TURKEY GIBLETS A LA BOURGEOISE—The giblets of turkey consist of the pinions, feet, neck and gizzard. After having scalded pick them well and put in a saucepan with a piece of butter, some parsley, green onions, clove of garlic, sprig of thyme, bay-leaf, a spoonful of flour moistened with stock, salt and pepper. Brown to a good color.

TURKEY TRUFFLES—Take a fat turkey, clean and singe it. Take three or four pounds of truffles, chopping up a handful with some fat bacon and put into a saucepan, together with the whole truffles, salt, pepper, spices and a bay-leaf. Let these ingredients cook over a slow fire for three-quarters of a hour, take off, stir and let cool. When quite cold place in body of turkey, sew up the opening and let the turkey imbibe the flavor of the truffles by remaining in a day or two, if the season permits. Cover the bird with slices of bacon and roast.

ANCHOVY STUFFING—Put some large fine chopped onions into a frying pan with a little oil or butter and fry them to a light brown. Put them in a basin and add some bread-crumbs that have been dipped in water and squeeze quite dry. Then add a small piece of liver of the bird to be stuffed. The filling of seven or eight salted anchovies, a pinch of parsley, with a few chopped capers. Work these well together, sprinkle over a little pepper and thicken the mixture with yolks of eggs, when it is ready for use.

CHESTNUT STUFFING—Peel a sound good-sized shallot, chop it up fine, place it in a saucepan on a hot fire with one table-spoonful of butter and heat it for three minutes without browning. Then add one-four pound of sausage meat and cook for five minutes longer. Add ten finely chopped mushrooms and a dozen well pounded cooked peeled chestnuts and stir all well together, season with one pinch of salt, half inch of pepper, one-half salt-spoon of powdered thyme, and one teaspoonful of finely chopped parsley. Let this come to a boil, add one half ounce of sifted bread crumbs and twenty-five or thirty whole cooked and shelled chestnuts and mix all well together, being careful not to break the chestnuts. Allow to cool and then is ready for use.

CHESTNUT STUFFING FOR TURKEY—Put a dozen or fifteen large chestnuts into a saucepan of water, and boil them until they are quite tender, then take off the shells and skins, put into a mortar and pound them. Put four ounces of shredded beef suet into a basin, stir in one-half pound of bread crumbs, season with salt and pepper to taste, and squeeze in a little lemon juice. Mix in a pound of chestnuts and stuffing will be ready for use.

CHESTNUT STUFFING WITH TRUFFLES—Remove the dark or outer skins from some chestnuts, immerse in boiling water for a few minutes, remove the light skins and boil for about twenty minutes, put in a saucepan one pound of fat bacon and two shallots, and keep these over the fire for a few minutes. Then add the whole chestnuts, also one-half pound of chestnuts previously cut out into small pieces, put in pepper, spices and salt to taste, and a small quantity of powdered margoram and thyme. Hold it over the fire a little longer, turning it occasionally. It is then ready for use.

CHICKEN LIVER STUFFING FOR BIRDS—Chop a half pound of fat chicken livers in small pieces and put them in a frying pan, with two finely chopped shallots, two ounces of fat ham, also chopped thyme, grated nutmeg, pepper, salt and a small lump of butter. Toss it about over the fire until partly cooked. Then take it off and leave it until cold. Pound in a mortar, then it is ready to use.

CHICKEN STUFFING—Take the heart, liver, and gizzard of a fowl, chop fine, season to taste and mix with boiled rice, worked up with a little butter. Stuff the chicken with this.

GIBLET STUFFING FOR TURKEY—Put the giblets in a saucepan over the fire with boiling water to cover, sprinkle over a teaspoonful of salt and a quarter of a teaspoonful of pepper and boil gently until tender. Save the water in which the giblets were boiled to use for gravy. Chop the giblets quite fine, put them in a frying pan over the fire with four ounces of butter, two breakfast cups of stale breadcrumbs and a good seasoning of salt, pepper and any powdered sweet herbs except sage. Stir all these ingredients together until they are of a light brown, add a wine glass of sherry or Madeira wine, and the force meat is ready for use.

PICKLED PORK STUFFING FOR TURKEYS—Chop up very fine a quarter of a pound of fat and lean salted pork, break quite fine a couple of breakfast cupfuls of bread and put them in a frying pan over the fire with two heaping tablespoonfuls of butter, fry to a brown and season with salt, pepper and any sweet herbs except sage.

POTATO STUFFING—Cut some peeled raw potatoes into slices of moderate thickness and then cut into squares, rinse with cold water, drain and place them in a saucepan with a couple of ounces of butter, a chopped onion and one or two tablespoonfuls of chopped parsley, a little salt and pepper and grated nutmeg, place the lid on the pan, keeping the pan at the side of the fire and shaking contents occasionally until nearly cooked, then chop fine an equal quantity of pig's liver and stir into the potatoes a few minutes before serving.

STUFFING FOR BIRDS—Peel two large onions, parboil them, then drain and chop them fine. Soak one breakfast cup of bread crumbs in as much milk as they will absorb without becoming too soft. Pour four ounces of butter in a stew-pan, place it over the fire, and when the butter is melted put in the onions, bread-crumbs and one tablespoon of chopped parsley, pepper and salt to taste. Add a small quantity of grated nutmeg. Add the beaten yolks of two eggs and stir the mixture over the fire until it is reduced to a paste, without allowing it to boil. The stuffing is then ready. It can be made in larger or smaller quantities according to the number of the birds to be stuffed.

STUFFING FOR BOILED TURKEY OR RABBIT—Remove the outer peel of one pound of chestnuts, then put them in boiling water until the inner skins can easily be removed, then trim them and put them into small lined saucepan, cover them with broth and boil until the pulp and the broth has been well reduced. Pass the chestnuts through a fine wire sieve. Chop fine one-fourth pound of cold boiled fat bacon and mix it with the chestnut puree, season to taste with salt, pepper and minced lemon peel. The stuffing will then be ready to serve.

STUFFING FOR DUCKS—Peel a fair size onion and sour cooking apple, chop them both very fine, and mix them with six ounces of finely grated stale breadcrumbs, one scant tablespoonful of sage leaves either powdered or finely mixed, one tablespoon butter, a little salt and butter. Bind the whole together with a beaten egg and it is then ready for the ducks.

STUFFING FOR FISH—Weigh two pounds of breadcrumbs without the crusts, and cut it into small squares, mix in one-half tablespoon of powdered curry and a liberal quantity of salt and pepper. Dissolve six ounces of butter in one-half pint of warm water and beat in the yolks of four eggs. Pour the liquid mixture over the bread and stir it well, but do not mash it. It is then ready to serve.

STUFFING FOR FOWLS—Trim off the crusts from two pounds of bread, put the crumbs into a basin of cold water, soak it for five minutes then turn it onto a sieve and drain well, press-ing out the water with a plate. When nearly dry cut the bread into small squares and season it well with powdered sage, salt and pepper. Warm one breakfast cupful of butter, beat in an egg and three teacupfuls of warm water and pour it over the bread, stirring it lightly, but not mashing it. Allow it to soak for ten minutes and the stuffing will then be ready to serve.

STUFFING FOR GOOSE—Roast fifty chestnuts, using care not to let them burn, remove the inner and outer peels and chop them fine. Chop the goose's liver, put it in a saucepan with one-half tablespoonful of chopped parsley, shallots, chives, and a little garlic and about two ounces of butter, fry them for a few minutes, then put in the chopped chestnuts with one pound of sausage meat, and fry the whole for fifteen minutes longer. The stuffing is then ready for use.

STUFFING FOR POULTRY—Put two handfuls of rice into a saucepan of water and parboil it, mix in ten or twelve chestnuts peeled or cut into small slices, one pan full of pistachio nuts and one handful of currants. Put the mixture in a saucepan with four ounces of butter, stir it well over the fire until thoroughly incorporated, season with pepper and salt and if liked a little ground cinnamon, and it is then ready for use. This stuffing is used for turkeys and other birds or anything else that is roasted whole.

STUFFING FOR POULTRY GALANTINE—Cut into squares three pounds of cooked flesh of either ducks or fowls; peel and chop two hard boiled eggs and one medium-size onion. Mix all of these together with three breakfast cupfuls of stale breadcrumbs, three well beaten eggs and one-half cupful of poultry fat that has been warmed; season to taste with pepper, salt and sage. After the force meat has been spread in the boned duck, or other bird, about one cupful of chopped jelly strewn over it will be an improvement and will set in the force meat.

STUFFING FOR RABBITS—Peel two onions and boil, when they are tender drain and mince them. Chop one-half pound pickled pork and few fine herbs, stir them in with the onions, then stir in the yolks of two eggs and add a sufficient quantity breadcrumbs to make it fairly consistent. Season to taste with pepper and salt, using a very little of the latter on account of the salt in the pork. Then stuffing is ready for use.

STUFFING FOR A SUCKLING PIG AND 'POSSUM—Put two tablespoonfuls of finely chopped onions into a saucepan with one teaspoon of oil. Toss them over the fire for five or six minutes, add eight ounces of rice boil in stock, an equal quantity of sausage meat, four or five ounces of butter, a small quantity of mince parsley, and pepper and salt to taste. Turn the mixture into a basin and add three eggs to make the whole into a stiff paste. It is then ready for use.

STUFFING FOR TURKEY (ROASTED)—To one pound of sifted breadcrumbs add one-half pound of butter, one pound of boiled and mashed potatoes and a little summer savory rubbed to a fine powder, add sufficient eggs to stiffen and season with salt, pepper and grated nutmeg. A little sausage meat, grated ham and a few oysters or chopped mushrooms may be added; they are a marked improvement, as are also a few walnuts roasted, chestnuts and filberts, and the same may also be served in the gravy with the bird.

STUFFING FOR VEAL—Trim off the skin and mince fine one-fourth pound of beef suet. Mix with it one cupful of bread crumbs, one tablespoonful of chopped parsley, two tablespoons of finely minced ham and the grated peel of a lemon. Season the stuffing to taste with pepper and salt and bind it with one beaten egg. It is then ready to use.

TRUFFLE AND CHESTNUT STUFFING—Peel off the thick outer skin of the chestnuts, put them into a saucepan with a bay leaf, a lump of salt, and plenty of coriander seeds. Cover them with water, and boil until nearly tender. Drain the chestnuts and peel off the inner skin, for every half pound of chestnuts, weighed after they are boiled and peeled, allow one-half pound of bacon, one-quarter pound of truffles, and the chestnuts all cut up into small pieces; season to taste with salt, pepper and spices and add a little each of powdered thyme and marjoram; toss the mixture for a few minutes longer over the fire and it is then ready for use.

TRUFFLE STUFFING FOR TURKEY—Brush well one and one-half pounds of truffles, peel them, mince the peel very fine, cut the truffles into slices, put them all into a saucepan with one-quarter pound of minced fat bacon and any obtainable fat from the turkey. Also a good size lump of butter, with salt and pepper to taste. Cook for ten minutes and let it get cold before using. A turkey should be stuffed with this three days before it is cooked, and truffle sauce should accompany it.

ENGLISH STUFFING—First, take some stale bread (use your own judgment as to the quantity), and brown it in your oven. Also one onion (red ones preferred), a quarter of a pound of fresh pork, or sausages, and run it through your meat grinder with a few stalks of celery; place it in a saucepan, in which a small lump of butter has been dissolved. Beat one or two

DINING FARE

Oysters Raw ....50 ¢

Fried and Roast ....60 ¢

Cold Beef Tongue, Sugar-Cured Ham,
Pressed Corned Beef, Sardines ....40 ¢

Chicken Salad, Lobster Salad ....50 ¢

Broiled Beefsteak with Potatoes ....60 ¢

Mutton Chops with Potatoes ....60 ¢

Ham with Potatoes ....50 ¢

Eggs Broiled, Fried,
Scrambled, Omelet, Plain ....40 ¢

Omelet with Rum ....50 ¢

Chow-Chow, Pickles
Welsh Rarebit ....50 ¢

French Coffee ....25 ¢

Tea ....25 ¢

IN 1868, TRAVELERS FROM CHICAGO TO NEW YORK COULD
CHOOSE AMONG THESE PULLMAN DINING CAR OFFERINGS.

TRAINS STOPPED AT ESTABLISHMENTS SUCH AS THIS ONE BEFORE PULLMAN OFFERED "IN TRANSIT" DINING THAT RIVALED THE FINEST RESTAURANTS IN NEW YORK. *Photographer and date unknown.*

eggs in a pint of sweet milk. Stir all ingredients well. Place on the fire or in the oven and continue to stir, so as to see that the onions are cooked. After you have this done set in a cool place; when the above articles are cold, place inside the turkey. Your seasoning that you place in the turkey, or make your gravy with, is sufficient. Roast it in the same way as you have done in the past.

LUNCH DISHES

BREAD, WITH CREAM CHEESE FILLING—For this use the steamed Boston brown bread and a potato loaf of white. Take the crust from the white loaf, using a sharp knife. Then instead of cutting crosswise cut in thin lengthwise pieces. Treat the brown loaf in the same way. Butter a slice of the white bread on one side and do the same with a brown slice. Put the two buttered sides together with a thin layer of fresh cream cheese between. Next butter the top of the brown slice of bread, spread again with cream cheese and lay a second slice of buttered white bread on top. Repeat until there are five layers, having the white last. Now with a sharp knife cut crosswise in thin slices. Sometimes the cream cheese filling can be varied with chopped pistachio nuts or olives, or it can be omitted entirely. In any case, it is delicate and appetizing.

CHEESE CROQUETTES—Cut one pound of American cheese into small dice. Have ready a cupful of very hot cream sauce, made by blending a tablespoonful each of flour and butter, and when melted adding a scant cup of hot milk. Stir until smooth and thickened. Add the cheese to this sauce, also the yolks of two eggs diluted with a little cream. Stir the whole and let it remain on the stove a moment until the cheese gets "steady." Season with salt, red and white pepper, and just a grating of nutmeg. Put this mixture on the ice until cold, then form into small croquettes and roll in fine bread or cracker crumbs. Dip in beaten egg, then again roll in the crumbs, drop into boiling fat and cook to a golden brown.

CHICKEN AND PIMENTO SANDWICHES—Add to finely minced chicken, roasted or boiled, an equal amount of pimentos. Moisten with mayonnaise and spread between wafer thin slices of white or brown bread. A leaf of lettuce may also be added.

CRESS SANDWICHES—Take thin slices of rare roast beef and cut into small pieces. Add an equal quantity of minced watercress dressed with a teaspoonful of grated horseradish, a little salt and paprika to season, and enough softened butter or thick cream to moisten. Blend the ingredients well, and spread between thin slices of buttered graham or whole wheat bread. Cut in neat triangles, but do not reject the crust.

BANANA SANDWICHES—Remove the skin and fibers from four bananas, cut them in quarters and force through a ricer. Mix with the pulp the juice of half a lemon, a dash of salt and nutmeg and set it away to become very cold while you prepare the bread. This should be cut in very thin slices, freed from crusts and trimmed into any preferred shape. Slightly sweeten some thick cream and add a speck of salt. Spread the bread with a thin layer of the cream, then with the banana pulp put together and wrap each in waxed paper, twist the ends, and keep very cold until serving time.

GERMAN RYE BREAD SANDWICHES—Put between buttered slices of rye bread chopped beef, cheese or chicken, and cover with finely chopped pickle, dill or the plain sour pickle. Another variation of the German sandwich is a layer of bologna sausage, then a thin layer of pumpernickle covered with another thin slice of rye bread. Cut into strips half an inch wide and the length of the slice.

GRILLED SARDINES ON TOAST—Drain the sardines and cook in a buttered frying-pan or chafing dish until heated, turning frequently. Place on oblong pieces of hot buttered toast, and serve.

HAM SANDWICHES—Chop two cups of ham, using a little fat with the lean. Mix one tablespoon of flour with enough cold water to make smooth, add one-half cup of boiling water, and cook five minutes; then add the ham and one teaspoon of dry mustard. Mix well and press into a bowl or jar.

JAPANESE SANDWICHES—These are made of any kind of left-over fish, baked, broiled or boiled. Pick out every bit of skin and bone, and flake in small pieces. Put into a saucepan with just a little milk or cream to moisten, add a little butter and a dusting of salt and pepper. Work to a paste while heating, then cool and spread on thin slices of buttered bread.

KEDGEREE—For this take equal quantities of boiled fish and boiled rice. For a cupful each use two hard boiled eggs, a teaspoonful curry powder, two tablespoonfuls butter, a half tablespoonful cream, and salt, white pepper and cayenne to season. Take all the skin and bone from the fish and put in a saucepan with the butter. Add the rice and whites of the boiled eggs cut fine, the cream, curry powder and cayenne. Toss over the fire until very hot, then take up and pile on a hot dish. Rub the yolks of the boiled eggs through a sieve on top of the curry, and serve.

SANDWICH FILLINGS—Other timely and appetizing fillings are green pepper and cucumber chopped fine and squeezed dry, then seasoned with mayonnaise, any of the potted and deviled meats seasoned with chopped parsley or cress with a teaspoonful creamed butter to make it spread, cheese and chopped spinach moistened with lemon juice and mayonnaise, veal chopped fine with celery or cress and mayonnaise. Camembert cheese heated slightly, just enough to spread, a Boston rarebit made with cream and egg left over scrambled eggs and cress, roast chicken and chopped dill pickles, cheese and chopped dates or figs, orange marmalade, and sardines pounded to a paste with a few drops of lemon juice added.

SANDWICHES FROM COLD MUTTON—Chop very fine, and to each pint add a tablespoonful of capers, a teaspoonful each chopped mint and salt, a dash of pepper, and a teaspoonful lemon juice. Spread thickly on buttered slices of whole wheat bread, cover with other slices of buttered bread, and cut in triangles.

TONGUE CANAPES—Cut bread into rounds, toast delicately, spread with potted tongue. In the centre put a stuffed olive and surround with a row of chopped beet and another of chopped white of egg.

CORN TOAST—Toast some slices of stale bread and butter, then pour over some canned corn, prepared as for the table, sprinkling a little pepper over it. If you have not already done so. Do not prepare so long before serving as to soak the bread too much. Peas are also good used the same way.

TONGUE TOAST—Mince boiled smoked tongue very fine, heat cream to the boiling point and make thick with the tongue. Season to taste with pepper, nutmeg, parsley or chopped green peppers and when hot stir in a beaten egg and remove from the fire at once. Have ready as many slices as are required, spread with the creamed tongue and serve at once. If you have no cream make a cream sauce, using a tablespoonful each of butter and flour and a cup of milk.

LUNCHEON SURPRISE—Line buttered muffin cups with hot boiled rice about half an inch thick. Fill the centers with minced cooked chicken seasoned with salt and pepper and a little broth or gravy. Cover the tops with rice and bake in a moderate oven for fifteen minutes. Unmold on a warm platter and serve with a cream sauce seasoned with celery salt. If liked, two or three oysters may be added to the filling in each cup.

SARDINE RAREBIT—One level tablespoon butter, one-fourth level teaspoon salt, one-fourth level teaspoon paprika, one level teaspoon mustard, one cup thin cream or milk, one cup grated cheese, one-fourth pound can sardines, boned and minced, two eggs, toast or crackers. Melt the butter, add the salt, paprika, mustard, cream and cheese and cook over hot water, stirring until the cheese is melted. Then add the sardines and eggs slightly beaten. When thick and smooth serve on toast or crackers.

BANANA CROQUETTES—Remove skins and scrape bananas. Sprinkle with powdered sugar and moisten with lemon juice. Let stand twenty minutes; cut in halves crosswise. Dip in egg, then in fine cracker crumbs and fry in deep fat. When done drain on brown paper. Serve with lemon sauce.

BACON AND GREEN PEPPERS—Select firm green peppers, cut into rings, removing all the seeds. Soak for twenty minutes in salted ice water. Drain and dry and fry in the pan in which the bacon has cooked crisp. Keep the bacon hot meanwhile. When the peppers are tender heap them up in the center of a small platter and arrange the slices of bacon around them.

CHEESE RAMEKINS—Use two rounding tablespoons of grated cheese, a rounding tablespoon of butter, one-quarter cup of fine breadcrumbs, the same of milk, and a saltspoon each of mustard and salt, the yolk of one egg. Cook the crumbs in the milk until soft, add the stiffly beaten white of the egg. Fill china ramekins two-thirds full and bake five minutes. Serve immediately.

CHEESE TIMBALES—Crumble into timbale cups, alternate layers of bread and American cheese. Pour over them a mixture of eggs, milk, salt, pepper and mustard, allowing one egg and a tablespoonful of milk to each timbale. Cook in the oven or on top of the stove in a shallow pan of hot water, kept covered.

FRIED BANANAS—Peel some bananas and cut in halves crosswise, roll in flour and fry in deep hot fat. Set on end and pour a hot lemon sauce around them.

MINCED CABBAGE—Wash a cabbage and lay in cold water for half an hour. With a sharp knife cut it into strips or shreds, an inch long, then drop them into iced water. Beat a pint of cream very stiff. Drain the cabbage, sprinkle lightly with salt, and stir it into the whipped cream, turning and tossing until it is thoroughly coated with the white foam. The cabbage should be tender and crisp for this dish.

NUT HASH—Chop fine cold boiled potatoes and any other vegetables desired that happen to be on hand. Put them into a buttered frying-pan and heat quickly and thoroughly, salt to taste, then just before serving stir in lightly a large spoonful of nut meal for each person to be served.

PEANUT MEATOSE—Dissolve one cup of cornstarch in two cups of tomato juice, add two cups of peanut butter and two teaspoons of salt. Stir for five minutes, then pour into cans and steam for four or five hours.

REMNANTS OF HAM WITH PEAS—Cut the ham into small cubes, measure and add an equal quantity of peas. In using canned peas rinse them well with cold water and drain. Mix the peas and ham and for one and one-half cups add a cup of white sauce seasoned with a teaspoon of lemon juice, a dash each of nutmeg and cayenne and salt to taste. Mix well and add one egg well beaten. Turn into a buttered baking dish, cover with buttered breadcrumbs and bake in a hot oven until well browned.

SCOTCH CNIPE—Four slices bread buttered, one-half box sardines (one-half pound size), five drops of onion juice, six drops lemon juice, few grains salt, two level teaspoons grated cheese, one tablespoon thick cream. Remove the skins and bones from the sardines, mince fine and add seasonings, cheese and cream. Mix to a paste, spread on bread and heat thoroughly in the oven.

SQUASH FLOWER OMELET—Put to soak in cold water. Then boil about fifteen minutes, strain in a colander and cut up, not too fine. Now a regular omelet is made but fried in a little bit of olive oil instead of butter, and just before it is turned over the flowers are spread on top. Brown quick and turn out on a hot platter.

VEGETABLE ROAST—Take cooked beans or peas, pass through a colander to remove the skins, and mix with an equal quantity of finely chopped nut meats. Season to taste. Put one-half the mixture into a buttered baking dish, spread over it a dressing made as follows: Pour boiling water on four slices of zwieback, cover, let stand for a few minutes, then break them up with a fork and pour over one-half cup of sweet cream, season with salt and sage. Cover the dressing with the remainder of the nut mixture, pour over all one-half cup of cream, and bake for one and one-half hours. Serve in slices with cranberry sauce.

WALNUT LOAF—One pint of dry breadcrumbs, one and one-half cups of chopped or ground nut meats, mix well with salt and sifted sage to suit the taste, add two tablespoons of butter, one beaten egg and sufficient boiling water to moisten. Form into a loaf and bake in a granite or earthen dish in a modern hot oven.

GAME, GRAVY AND GARNISHES

ROASTED CANVAS-BACK DUCK—Procure a fine canvas-back duck, pick, singe, draw thoroughly and wipe; throw inside a light pinch of salt, run in the head from the end of the head to the back, press and place in a roasting pan. Sprinkle with salt, put in a brisk oven, and cook for eighteen minutes. Arrange on a very hot dish, untruss, throw in two tablespoons of white broth. Garnish with slices of fried hominy and currant jelly. Redhead and mallard ducks are prepared the same way.

BROILED WILD DUCK—Pick, singe and draw well a pair of wild ducks, split them down the back without detaching, place them skin downwards on a dish, season with salt and pepper and pour over two tablespoons of oil. Boil the birds well in this marinade, place them on a broiler on a brisk fire, broil for seven minutes on each side. Place them on a hot dish and cover with maitre d'hotel butter, garnish with watercress, and serve.

ROAST DUCK WITH ORANGE SAUCE—Scrape a tablespoonful each of fat, bacon, and raw onion and fry them together for five minutes. Add the juice of an orange and a wineglassful of port wine, the drippings from the duck and seasoning of salt and pepper. Keep hot without boiling and serve with roast duck.

"The wild geese must have heard him call,
for they flew back to see if he was coming."

From "The Wonderful Adventures of Nils" in
The Winston Readers Third Reader.

Illustration by Frederick Richardson in 1918

Written by Sidney G. Firman and Ethel H. Maltby.

THANKSGIVING POSTCARD, DATE UNKNOWN, READS "WHY SHOULDN'T I BE THANKFUL? /
I'D RATHER EAT SOME NICE FOWL / THAN TO BE ONE, BIG AND FAT. /
AND SO WITH ALL MY HEART TODAY / I'M THANKFUL FOR THAT."

CHICKEN GRAVY—Put into a stockpot the bones and trimmings of a fowl or chicken with a small quantity of stock and boil them. Add flour and butter to thicken it, and then place the pot on the side of the stove and let simmer. Stir well and after the gravy has simmered for some minutes skim and strain it, and it will be ready to serve.

GRAVY FOR WILD FOWL—Put into a small saucepan a blade of mace, piece of lemon peel, two tablespoonfuls each of mushroom catsup, walnut catsup and strained lemon juice, two shallots cut in slices, two wineglasses of port wine. Put the pan over the fire and boil the contents; then strain, add it to the gravy that has come from the wild fowl while roasting. If there is a large quantity of gravy less wine and catsup will be necessary.

SALMI OF GAME—Cut cold roast partridges, grouse or quail into joints and lay aside while preparing the gravy. This is made of the bones, dressing, skin, and general odds and ends after the neatest pieces of the birds have been selected. Put this (the scraps) into a saucepan, with one small onion minced, and a bunch of sweet herbs, pour in a pint of water and whatever gravy may be left, and stew, closely covered, for nearly an hour. A few bits of pork should be added if there is no gravy. Skim and strain, return to the fire, and add the juice of a half lemon, with a pinch of nutmeg, thicken with browned flour if the stuffing has not thickened it sufficiently, boil up and pour over the reserved meat, which should be put into another saucepan. Warm until smoking hot, but do not let it boil. Arrange the pieces of bird in heap upon a dish and pour the gravy over them.

LENTEN DISHES

ORANGE FOOL—Take the juice of six oranges, six eggs well beaten, a pint of cream, quarter of a pound of sugar, little cinnamon and nutmeg. Mix well together. Place over a slow fire and stir until thick, then add a small lump of butter.

PLUM PORRIDGE—Take a gallon of water, half a pound of barley, quarter of a pound of raisins, and a quarter of a pound of currants. Boil until half the water is wasted. Sweeten to taste and add half pint of white wine.

RICE SOUP—Boil two quarts of water and a pound of rice, with a little cinnamon, until the rice is tender. Take out the cinnamon and sweeten rice to taste. Grate half a nutmeg over it and let stand until it is cold. Then beat up the yolks of three eggs, with half a pint of white wine, mix well and stir into the rice. Set over a slow fire, stirring constantly to prevent curdling. When it is of good thickness it is ready to serve.

RICE MILK—Boil half pound of rice in a quart of water, with a little cinnamon. Let it boil until the water is wasted, taking great care it does not burn. Then add three pints of milk and the yolk of an egg. Beat up and sweeten to taste.

FORCED MEAT BALLS FOR TURTLE SOUP—Cut off a very small part of the vealy part of a turtle, mince it very fine and mix it with a very small quantity of boned anchovy and boiled celery, the yolks of one or two hard-boiled eggs, and two tablespoons of sifted breadcrumbs, with mace, cayenne pepper and salt to taste, a small quantity of warm butter, and well beaten egg. Form the paste into balls, plunge them into a frying-pan of boiling butter or fat, fry them to a good color, and they are ready. They should be added to the soup hot.

TRUFFLES FOR GARNISH—Choose large round truffles, wash them thoroughly and peel them, and put the required number into a saucepan, pour over them enough chicken broth or

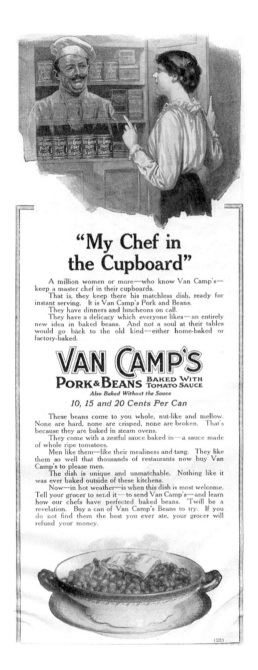

"My Chef in the Cupboard"

A million women or more—who know Van Camp's—keep a master chef in their cupboards.

That is, they keep there his matchless dish, ready for instant serving. It is Van Camp's Pork and Beans.

They have dinners and luncheons on call.

They have a delicacy which everyone likes—an entirely new idea in baked beans. And not a soul at their tables would go back to the old kind—either home-baked or factory-baked.

VAN CAMP'S
PORK & BEANS BAKED WITH TOMATO SAUCE
Also Baked Without the Sauce

10, 15 and 20 Cents Per Can

These beans come to you whole, nut-like and mellow. None are hard, none are crisped, none are broken. That's because they are baked in steam ovens.

They come with a zestful sauce baked in—a sauce made of whole ripe tomatoes.

Men like them—like their mealiness and tang. They like them so well that thousands of restaurants now buy Van Camp's to please men.

The dish is unique and unmatchable. Nothing like it was ever baked outside of these kitchens.

Now—in hot weather—is when this dish is most welcome. Tell your grocer to send it—to send Van Camp's—and learn how our chefs have perfected baked beans. 'Twill be a revelation. Buy a can of Van Camp's Beans to try. If you do not find them the best you ever ate, your grocer will refund your money.

(331)

ADVERTISEMENT FOR VAN CAMP'S PORK AND BEANS FROM *Modern Priscilla* MAGAZINE AUGUST, 1914. GILBERT C. VAN CAMP SECURED AN ARMY CONTRACT DURING THE CIVIL WAR THAT HELPED MAKE VAN CAMP'S PORK AND BEANS A STAPLE FOR UNION TROOPS.

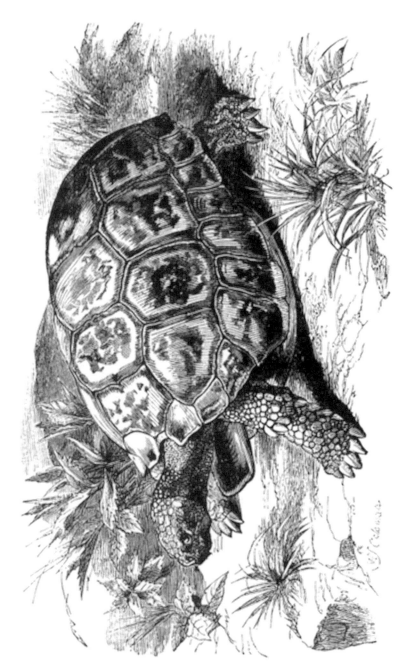

CHARMING ILLUSTRATION FROM LATE 1800S OF THE MAJOR INGREDIENT IN MR. ESTES' "FORCED MEAT BALLS FOR TURTLE SOUP" RECIPE.

Illustrator unknown

champagne to nearly cover them, add an onion stuck with three or four cloves, a clove of garlic, a bunch of sweet herbs, and a little of the skimmings of the chicken broth or fat. Place the pan on the fire and boil for fifteen minutes with the lid on, then remove from the fire, and let the truffles cool in their liquor. Remove them, drain, and they are ready for use. Another way to fix them is to boil them ten minutes and cut them into various shapes. The trimmings from them as well as the liquor may be used in making sauce.

FRIED PARSLEY—Carefully pick the stems from the parsley, dry it on a cloth, put into a frying basket, then into hot fat. Be careful that the fat is not too hot. Fry for a few minutes.

BEEF MARROW QUENELLES—Put one-half pound beef marrow into a basin, with an equal quantity of breadcrumbs, add two tablespoons of flour; salt and pepper to taste. Work it into a smooth paste with the yolks of six eggs and the whites of one. Take it out a little at a time and poach in boiling salted water, drain, trim, and serve very hot.

CALF'S LIVER QUENELLES—Steep a thick layer of bread in milk, until well soaked, then squeeze and mix with half a pound of finely ground calf's liver, and season with parsley, chives and lemon peel in small quantities, and all finely ground. Dust in salt and pepper and a tablespoonful of flour. Bind the mixture with beaten eggs. Divide the mixture with a tablespoon into small quantities and shape each one like an oval. Plunge the ovals into a saucepan of boiling water and boil for a half an hour. Chop some bacon, place it in a frying-pan with a lump of butter and fry until brown. When the quenelles are cooked pour the hot bacon and fat over them, and serve.

CHICKEN QUENELLES—Mix together one teacupful each of breadcrumbs and finely pounded cooked chicken. Season highly with salt and cayenne and bind with raw egg yolks. Mold into pieces about the size and shape of an olive, between two spoons. Roll in egg and cracker dust and fry them, or poach them in boiling broth or water until they float, and use them as desired.

MISCELLANEOUS

BEAUREGARD EGGS—Two level tablespoons butter, two level tablespoons flour, one-half level teaspoon salt, one cup milk, four hard-boiled eggs. Make a white sauce of the butter, flour, salt and milk, and add the whites of the eggs chopped fine. Cut buttered toast in pointed pieces and arrange on a hot plate to form daisy petals. Cover with the sauce and put the egg yolks through a ricer into the center.

EGG AND POTATO SCALLOP—Fill a buttered baking dish with alternate layers of cold boiled potatoes sliced thin, hard-boiled eggs also sliced, and a rich white sauce poured over each layer. Cover the top with buttered crumbs and set in the oven until the crumbs are browned.

EGGS SCRAMBLED IN MILK—Half pint of milk, five eggs. Heat the milk in a saucepan and when it is just at the boiling point stir in the eggs, which should have been beaten enough to mix them thoroughly. Stir steadily until they thicken, add a half teaspoonful of salt and serve at once.

EGG WITH WHITE SAUCE FOR LUNCHEON—Cut stale bread into one-fourth slices and shape into rounds, then saute in olive oil. Arrange on a hot platter and on each place a French poached egg. Cover with Marnay sauce, sprinkle with buttered breadcrumbs and put in oven just long enough to brown crumbs. For the Marnay sauce, cook one and one-half cups of chicken stock with one slice of onion, one slice carrot, bit of bay leaf, a sprig of parsley and six peppercorns until reduced to one cup, then strain. Melt one-fourth cup of butter, add one-fourth cup flour, and stir until well blended, then pour on gradually while constantly heating the chicken stock and three-fourths cup scalded milk. Bring to the boiling point and add one-half teaspoon salt, one-eighth teaspoon paprika, two tablespoons of Parmesean cheese and one-half cup goose or duck liver, cut in one-third inch cubes.

"ALI BABA AND THE FORTY THIEVES."

"ALI BABA AND THE FORTY THIEVES"
CREAM OF WHEAT AD FROM 1914

"MAKING MAPLE SYRUP IN THE GOOD OLD FASHIONED WAY,"
FROM 1906

Photograph courtesy of The Library of Congress.

LIGHT OMELET—Separate your eggs and beat the yolks until thick and light colored, adding a tablespoonful cold water for each yolk and a seasoning of salt and pepper. Beat the whites until they are dry and will not slip from the dish, then turn into them the beaten yolks, folding carefully until thoroughly blended. Have the pan hot and butter melted, turn in the mixture, smothering it over the top, cover and place on asbestos mat on top of stove until well risen, then uncover and set in the oven to dry. Try it with a heated silver knife thrust in the middle. When done, cut across the middle, fold and turn out, dust with sugar, glaze and serve quickly.

OMELET FOR ONE—Beat the yolks of two eggs until creamy, add four tablespoons of milk and salt-spoon of salt. Add the whites beaten stiff and put into a hot pan in which a rounding teaspoon of butter is melted. The mixture should begin to bubble almost at once; cook three or four minutes, slipping a knife under now and then to keep the under side from burning. When the top begins to set, fold it over and turn on a hot platter.

SCRAMBLED EGGS WITH MUSHROOMS—Pare, wash and slice half a pound of fresh mushrooms, put them in a sautoir; cover, shake the sautoir once in awhile and cook ten minutes. Break and beat five or six eggs in a saucepan, adding seasoning of salt, pepper, nutmeg and one-half ounces of butter cut into bits. Add the mushrooms, set over the fire, stir constantly with wooden paddle, and when eggs are thick and creamy turn into a heated dish, garnish with toasted bread points, and serve at once.

SCRAMBLED EGGS WITH PEPPERS—Scrambled eggs on toast with chopped sweet green peppers make an excellent breakfast dish. Toast four slices of bread, butter, and put where the platter on which they are arranged will keep hot. Put a tablespoonful of butter in a hot frying-pan, as soon as it bubbles turn in half a dozen eggs which have been broken into a bowl, and mix with half a dozen tablespoonfuls of water. As the whites begin to set, whip together quickly with a silver knife. Sprinkle over the top two finely cut peppers from which the seeds have been removed, stir through the eggs, let the whole cook a half minute, then pour over the slices of toast, garnish with sprigs of parsley, and serve at once.

SCOTCH EGGS—Shell six hard-boiled eggs and cover with a paste made of one-third stale breadcrumbs cooked soft in one-third cup milk, then mix with one cup lean boiled ham minced very fine and seasoned with cayenne pepper, one-half teaspoon mixed mustard and one raw egg beaten. Roll slightly in fine breadcrumbs and fry in hot deep fat a delicate brown.

BANANAS WITH OATMEAL—Add a teaspoonful of salt to a quart of rapidly boiling water and sprinkle in two cups of rolled oatmeal. Set the saucepan into another dish of boiling water (double boiler), cover and cook at least one hour. Longer cooking is preferable. Have ready half a banana for each person to be served. The banana should be peeled and cut in thin slices. Put a spoonful of the hot oatmeal over the bananas in the serving dishes. Pass at the same time sugar and milk or cream. Other cereals may be served with bananas in the same way.

SPAWN AND MILK—Have the water boiling fast. Salt to taste, then holding a handful of meal high in the left hand, let it sift slowly between the fingers into the bubbling water, stirring all the time with the right hand. Stir until a thin, smooth consistency obtains, then push back on the fire where it will cook slowly for several hours, stirring occasionally with a "pudding stick" or wooden spoon. It will thicken as it cooks. Serve in bowls with plenty of good rich milk.

BOILED SAMP—Soak two cupfuls over night in cold water. In the morning wash thoroughly, cover with boiling water, and simmer gently all day. Do not stir, as that tends to make it mushy, but shake the pot frequently. As the water boils away add more, but not enough to make much liquid. About a half hour before serving add a cupful rich milk, tablespoon butter, and salt to season. Let this boil up once, and serve hot.

MOLDED CEREAL WITH BANANA SURPRISE—Turn any left-over breakfast cereal, while still hot, into cups rinsed in cold water, half filling the cups. When cold, scoop out the centers and fill the open spaces with sliced bananas, turn from the cups onto a buttered agate pan, fruit downward, and set into a hot oven to become very hot. Remove with a broad-bladed knife to cereal dishes. Serve at once with sugar and cream or milk.

THICKENED BUTTER—Place in a saucepan the yolks of a couple of eggs. Break them gently with a spoon, adding four ounces of butter, melted but not browned. Set the pan over a slow fire, stirring until of the required consistency.

SHRIMP BUTTER—Pick and shell one pound of shrimps, place them in a mortar and pound, add one-half pound of butter when well mixed; pass the whole through a fine sieve. The butter is then ready for use.

SARDINE BUTTER—Remove the skins and bones from seven or eight sardines, put them in a mortar and pound until smooth. Boil two large handfuls of parsley until tender, squeeze it as dry as possible, remove all stalks and stems and chop it. Put the parsley in the mortar with the fish and four ounces of butter, then pound again. When well incorporated mold the butter into shapes. Keep on ice until ready for serving. Excellent for hot toast.

MAITRE D'HOTEL BUTTER—Quarter of a pound of butter, two tablespoonfuls of chopped parsley, salt and pepper and juice of two lemons. Mix thoroughly and keep in cool place.

CAULIFLOWER IN MAYONNAISE—Select some large, cold boiled cauliflowers and break into small branches, adding a little salt, pepper and vinegar to properly season. Heap them on a dish to form a point. Surround with a garnish of cooked carrots, turnips and green vegetables, pour some white mayon-naise sauce over all, and serve.

SARDINE COCKTAIL—Drain and skin one-half box boneless sardines and separate into small pieces. Add one-half cup tomato catsup, mixed with two teaspoons Worcestershire sauce, one-half teaspoon tabasco sauce, the juice of one lemon, and salt to taste. Chill thoroughly and serve in scallop shells, placing each shell on a plate of crushed ice.

SAUCE FOR VARIOUS SHELLFISH IN THE SHAPE OF COCKTAIL—For the truffle sauce melt three tablespoons of butter, add three tablespoons of flour, and stir until well blended, then pour on gradually while heating constantly one cup milk and one-half cup heavy cream. Bring to the boiling point and add two chopped truffles, two tablespoons Madeira wine, salt and pepper to taste.

BAKED MILK—Put fresh milk into a stone jar, cover with white paper and bake in a moderate oven until the milk is thick as cream. This may be taken by the most delicate stomach.

MINT VINEGAR—Fill in a wide-mouthed bottle or a quart fruit jar with fresh mint leaves, well washed and bruised a little. Let the leaves fall in without pressing. Fill the jar with cider vinegar, put on the rubber, and turn the cover tightly. Let stand three weeks, uncover, and drain off the vinegar into bottles and keep well corked.

BLACKBERRY VINEGAR—Mash the berries to a pulp in an earthenware or wooden vessel. Add good cider vinegar to cover and stand in sun during the day and in the cellar at night, stirring occasionally. Next morning strain and add the same amount fresh berries. Crush and pour the whole, the strained juice, and set in the sun again all day and in the cellar at night. The third day strain to each quart of the juice one pint water and five pounds sugar. Heat slowly and when at boiling point skim, and after it boils strain and bottle.

HOMEMADE VINEGAR—For pineapple vinegar, cover the parings and some of the fruit, if you wish, with water. A stone crock or glass jar is the best receptacle for this purpose. Add sugar or sirup, according to the condition of the fruit, and set in the sun where it can ferment thoroughly. Skim frequently to remove all impurities, and when as acid as desired, strain and bottle. Gooseberry vinegar is made by crushing goose-berries not quite ripe, covering with cold water (three quarts of water to two or fruit) and allowing it to stand for two days. Press and strain. Allow a pint of sugar and half a yeast cake to each gallon of the liquid. Set in the sun, and when the fluid has worked clear, strain and leave in a warm place until as sharp as desired. A cloth should be tied over the top of the jar to keep out insects and dust.

SAMP AND BEANS—Soak a quart of the samp and a scant pint pea beans over night in cold water, each in a separate vessel. In the morning put the samp over to cook in a large pot, covering with fresh boiling water. Simmer gently about two hours, protecting from scorch, by an asbestos mat and a frequent shaking of the pot. As the samp commences to swell and the water dries out add more. After two hours add the beans that have been soaking, together with a pound of streaked salt pork. Season with salt and pepper and continue the cooking all day, shak-ing frequently. Just before serving add butter and more salt if it needs it.

DRESSING FOR ITALIAN RAVIOLI—Nine eggs beaten very light. One quart of spinach boiled and drained until dry. Chop very fine. Add salt and pepper to taste, one cup grated American cream cheese, little nutmeg, one-half pint breadcrumbs soaked in milk, two tablespoonfuls olive oil, three tablespoonfuls of cream. Cracker meal enough to thicken.

NOODLE DOUGH FOR ITALIAN RAVIOLI—Make noodle crust as you would for noodles. Roll very fine and cover half the crust with ravioli dressing half-inch thick. Turn over the other half to cover. Mark in squares as shown in figure.

Cut with a pie cutter after marking. Drop one by one in salted boiling water, cook about twenty minutes, drain and arrange on platter and sprinkle each layer with grated cheese and mushroom sauce.

BOLOGNA SAUSAGE—Chop fine one pound each of beef, pork, veal and fat bacon. Mix with three-fourths of a pound of fine chopped beef suet and season with sage, sweet herbs, salt and pepper. Press into large skins thoroughly cleaned and soaked in cold salt water for several hours before being used, fasten tightly on both ends and prick in several places. Place in a deep saucepan, cover with boiling water, simmer gently for an hour, lay on straw to dry and hang.

LEMON JELLY—Grate two lemons and the juice of one. The yolks of three eggs, two cups of sugar. Butter, the size of an egg. Boil until thick.

MARGARETTES—One half-pound of peanuts, one pound of dates chopped fine. One cup of milk in the dates and boil, add peanuts. Make a boiled icing. Take the long branch crackers, spread the filling between the crackers, put on the icing and put in the oven to brown.

VEGETABLES

BRUSSELS SPROUTS—Wash well in salted water about two pounds of Brussels sprouts and pick them over well. Place them on a fire in a saucepan filled with water, a little salt and bicarbonate of soda. With the lid off boil fast till tender; about twenty to twenty-five minutes. When done drain them and dry on a cloth. Put in a large saucepan a good-sized lump of butter and a little salt and pepper. Toss the sprouts in this until they become quite hot again, but do not fry them. Serve on a quartered round of buttered toast.

BRUSSELS SPROUTS MAITRE D'HOTEL—Boil the sprouts and then place them in a saucepan with a lump of butter and beat them well. Put half a pound of fresh butter in a pan with two tablespoonfuls of chopped parsley, the juice of a couple of lemons, a little salt and white pepper and mix together well with a spatula, and when it boils stir quickly. Place the sprouts on a dish and turn the sauce over them.

BRUSSELS SPROUTS SAUTED—One pound of Brussels sprouts should be thoroughly washed and boiled and then put into a pan over the fire together with a good-sized lump of butter, a little salt, and toss for eight minutes. Sprinkle over them a little chopped parsley, and serve when done.

BAKED MUSHROOMS IN CUPS—Peel and cut off the stalks of a dozen or more large fat mushrooms, and chop up fine. Put the trimmings in a stewpan with some water or clear gravy, and boil well. When nicely flavored strain the liquor, return it to the stewpan with the mushrooms and a moderate quantity of finely chopped parsley, season to taste with salt and pepper, and boil gently on the side of the stove for nearly three-quarters of an hour. Beat four eggs well in one-half teacupful of cream, and strain. When the mushrooms are ready move the stewpan away from the fire and stir in the beaten eggs. Butter some small cups or molds, fill each with the mixture, and bake in a

It comes to you
ready cooked

One of the
57

SINCE we started to cook Spaghetti in the Heinz kitchens four years ago the demand for Heinz Spaghetti has increased with such rapidity that it has become a great national dish.

Every family that once tries it will surely make it a regular dish. Ready-cooked, with the delicious Heinz tomato sauce and cheese, it makes an appeal to everyone's appetite. Wholesome, nutritious.

It is to be found in every grocery store.

HEINZ
Spaghetti

comes to you ready cooked
with Tomato Sauce and Cheese

All Heinz goods sold in Canada are made in Canada

Please mention THE ETUDE when addressing our advertisers.

IN THIS ADVERTISEMENT, HEINZ BRAGS ABOUT HOW POPULAR SPAGHETTI
HAS BECOME IN THE 4 YEARS SINCE THEY'VE BEEN MAKING IT.

From Presser's 1916 Musical Magazine The Etude.

" . . . WHEN HIS PA WAS FAST ASLEEP, HE QUICKLY DUMPED
HALF THE CONTENTS OF HIS BASKET INTO HIS OWN."

Illustration by Louise A. Field from the children's book Peter Rabbit and His Pa,
written by Virginia Albert, and published by the Saalfield Publishing Company in 1916.

brisk oven. Prepare some white sauce; when baked turn the mushrooms out of the molds on a hot dish, pour the sauce around them, and serve.

BOILED CHESTNUTS SERVED AS VEGETABLES— Peel off the outside skin of the chestnuts and steep them in boiling water until the skin can be easily removed, and throw them into a bowl of cold water. Put two ounces of butter into a saucepan with two tablespoons of flour and stir the whole over a fire until well mixed. Then pour in one-half pint or more of clear broth and continue stirring over the fire until it boils. Season with salt, throw in the chestnuts and keep them simmering at the side of the fire until tender. When served in this way they make a good vegetable for roasted meat or poultry, particularly turkey.

BOILED CORN—Choose short, thick ears of fresh corn, remove all the husks except the inner layer: strip that down far enough to remove the silk and any defective grains and then replace it, and tie at the upper end of each ear of corn. Have ready a large pot half full of boiling water, put in the corn and boil steadily for about twenty minutes, if the ears are large, and fifteen minutes if they are small. Remove from the boiling water, take off the strings, and serve hot at once. If desirable, the inner husk may be removed before serving, but this must be done very quickly, and the ears covered with a napkin or a clean towel to prevent the heat from escaping. Serve plenty of salt, butter and pepper with the corn. These may be mixed by heating them together, and serve in a gravy bowl.

BOILED ONIONS WITH CREAM—Peel twelve medium-sized onions, pare the roots without cutting them, place in a saucepan, cover with salted water, add a bunch of parsley, and boil for forty-five minutes; take them from the saucepan, place them on a dish, covering with two gills of cream sauce, mixed with two tablespoonfuls of broth, garnish, and serve.

CORN FRITTERS—Prepare four ears of fresh corn by removing the outer husks and silks; boil and then drain well. Cut the grains from the cobs and place in a bowl, season with salt and pepper, add one-fourth pound of sifted flour, two eggs and a half pint of cold milk. Stir vigorously, but do not beat, with a wooden spoon for five minutes, when it will be sufficiently firm; butter a frying-pan, place it on a fire, and with a ladle holding one gill put the mixture on the pan in twelve parts, being careful that they do not touch one another, and fry till of a good golden color, cooking for four or five minutes on each side. Dress them on a folded napkin, and serve.

BROILED EGGPLANT—Peel an eggplant and cut it into six slices each half an inch thick. Put them into a dish and season with salt and pepper and pour over them one tablespoon of sweet oil. Mix well and arrange the slices of the eggplant on a broiler and broil on each side for five minutes, then place on a dish which has been heated and pour over a gill of maitre d'hotel sauce, and serve.

FRIED EGGPLANT—Select a nice large eggplant, peel, remove the seeds, and cut into pieces about one and one-half inches long and three-quarters of an inch wide. Put them on a plate, sprinkle well with salt and leave standing for an hour or so. Then wrap the pieces in a cloth and twist it around so as to squeeze as much juice as possible from them without breaking. Sprinkle over with flour, covering each side well, and place them in a frying basket. Put a large lump of fat in a stewpan and when it boils put in the basket. As each plant is nicely browned take out of the basket, sprinkle with salt and lay on a sheet of paper in front of a fire so as to drain as free as possible from fat. Serve on a napkin spread over a hot dish.

EGGPLANT FRITTERS—Boil the eggplant in salted water mixed with a little lemon juice. When tender, skin, drain and mash them. For every pint of pulp, add one-half breakfast cup full of flour, two well beaten eggs, and season with salt and pepper to taste. Shape into fritters and fry in boiling fat until brown.

BROILED MUSHROOMS ON TOAST—Trim off the stalks of the required quantity of large mushrooms, peel, score them once across the top, place them on a gridiron and grill over a slow fire, turning when done on one side. Trim the crusts off some slices of bread and toast on both sides. Cut rounds out of the toast the same size as the mushrooms, butter them and place a mushroom on each. Put a lump of butter in each mushroom and sprinkle over with salt and pepper. Place a fancy dish-paper on a hot dish, and serve the mushrooms-on-toast, with a garnish of fried parsley.

DEVILED MUSHROOMS—Cut off the stalks even with the head and peel and trim the mushrooms neatly. Brush them over inside with a paste brush dipped in warm butter, and season with salt and pepper, and a small quantity of cayenne pepper. Put them on a gridiron and broil over a clear fire. When cooked put the mushrooms on a hot dish, and serve.

MUSHROOMS IN CREAM—Peel and trim the required quantity of mushrooms. Put some cream in a pan over the fire and season with pepper and salt to taste. Rub the mushrooms in salt and pepper, and as quickly as the cream comes to a boil put them in and let boil for four minutes. Serve hot.

BOILED SPANISH ONIONS—Boil Spanish onions in salted water thirty minutes. Drain and add butter or drippings, salt and pepper, covering the pan to prevent steam from escaping. Cook slowly for about three hours, basting frequently with drippings. Care should be taken that they do not burn.

BAKED ONIONS—Put six large onions into a saucepan of water, or water and milk in equal proportions, add salt and pepper and boil until tender. When done so they can be easily mashed work them up with butter to the consistency of paste, cover with breadcrumbs, and bake in a moderate oven. If preferred they may be boiled whole, put in a baking dish covered with butter and breadcrumbs, then baked.

FRIED ONIONS—Peel and slice into even rounds four medium-sized onions. Place them first in milk then in flour, fry in very hot fat for eight minutes. Remove them carefully and lay on a cloth to dry. Place a folded napkin on a dish, lay the onions on, and serve very hot. Garnish with fried parsley.

GLAZED ONIONS—Peel the onions and place in a saucepan with a little warmed butter, add sugar and salt to taste, pour over a little stock. Place over a moderate fire and cook slowly till quite tender and the outside brown. Remove and serve on a dish. A little of the liquor, thickened with flour, may be served as a sauce.

FRIED SPANISH ONIONS—Peel and slice two pounds of Spanish onions. Place them in a hot frying-pan, containing two heaping tablespoonfuls of butter, add salt and pepper.

BOILED OYSTER PLANT—Scrape a bunch of oyster plants, dropping into cold water to which a little vinegar has been added. Cut in small pieces and boil in salted water until tender. Season with butter, pepper and cream. Cream may be omitted if desired.

BROILED POTATOES—Peel a half dozen medium-sized cooked potatoes, halve them and lay upon a dish, seasoning with a pinch of salt, and pour over them two tablespoons of butter and roll them thoroughly in it. Then arrange them on a double broiler, and broil over a moderate fire for three minutes on each side. Serve in a folded napkin on a hot dish.

PARSNIP FRITTERS—Peel and boil some parsnips until tender, then drain thoroughly and mash, mixing in with them two beaten eggs, salt to taste, and sufficient flour to bind them stiffly. Divide and mold the mixture into small round cakes with floured hands. Put a large piece of butter into a stewpan, place on the fire and let it boil. Then put in the cakes and fry to a nice golden brown color. Take out and drain them, and serve on a napkin spread over a hot dish, with a garnish of fried parsley.

MASHED PARSNIPS—Wash and scrape some parsnips, cut in pieces lengthwise, put them in a saucepan with boiling water, a little salt and a small lump of drippings. Boil till tender, remove and place in a colander to drain, and press all the waste out of them. Mash them till quite smooth with a wooden spoon, put them in a saucepan with a tablespoonful of milk or a small lump of butter, and a little salt and pepper; stir over the fire until thoroughly hot again, turn out on to a dish, and serve immediately.

POTATO BALLS—Mash thoroughly a pound of boiled potatoes and rub them through a wire sieve. Mix in a quarter of a pound of grated ham, a little chopped parsley, and a small onion chopped very fine, together with a small quantity of grated nutmeg, and the beaten yolks of two eggs. Roll this mixture into balls of equal size, then roll in flour and egg-breadcrumbs, and fry in dripping or brown them in the oven, and serve on a hot dish.

POTATOES AND ONIONS SAUTED—Take an equal amount of small new potatoes and onions of equal size, peel and place in a saute pan with a good-sized piece of butter, tossing them over the fire for a quarter of an hour, being careful not to let them burn. Put in enough water to half cover the vegetables, add a little salt and pepper, place the lid over the pan and stew gently for half an hour, then squeeze a little lemon juice in it and turn on a hot dish, and serve.

POTATOES LYONNAISE—Cut into round slices eight boiled potatoes, lay in a frying-pan with an ounce and a half of butter and the round slices of a fried onion, seasoning with a pinch each of salt and pepper. Cook for six minutes, or until they become well browned, tossing them all the while. Sprinkle over with a small quantity of chopped parsley, and serve.

STEWED MUSHROOMS—Peel and remove the stalks from some large mushrooms, wash and cut them into halves; put two ounces of butter into a small lined saucepan with two tablespoonfuls of flour and stir this over the fire, then mix in by degrees one and one-half breakfast cupfuls of milk; while boiling and after being thickened, put in the mushrooms. Season to taste with salt, pepper and a small quantity of powdered mace, and stew gently on the side of the fire until tender. When cooked turn the mushrooms on to a hot dish, garnish with some croutons of bread that have been fried to a nice brown, and serve.

STUFFED ONIONS, STEAMED—Peel eight large onions and boil for ten minutes, and salt them slightly. Remove them from the fire, drain quite dry, push about half the insides out; chop the parts taken out very small, together with a little sausage meat; add one teacupful of breadcrumbs, one egg, and salt and pepper to taste. Put this mixture into the cavity in the onions, piling a little on the top and bottom so that none shall be left. Arrange them in a deep pan. Put them in a steamer over a saucepan of water and steam for one hour and a half. Put the pan in the oven to brown the tops of the onions, adding one breakfast cupful of butter to prevent burning. Arrange them tastefully on a dish, and serve hot.

POTATO CROQUETTES—Take four boiled potatoes and add to them half their weight in butter, the same quantity of powdered sugar, salt, grated peel of half a lemon and two well beaten eggs. Mix thoroughly and roll into cork-shaped pieces and dip into the beaten yolks of eggs, rolling in sifted breadcrumbs. Let stand one hour and again dip in egg and roll in crumbs. Fry in boiling lard or butter. Serve with a garnish of parsley.

CREAMED POTATOES—Cut into cubes or dices about half a pound of boiled potatoes and place in a shallow baking pan. Pour over them enough milk or cream to cover them and put in the oven or on the side of the stove and cook gently until nearly all the milk is absorbed. Add a tablespoonful of butter, a teaspoonful each of finely chopped parsley, and salt, and half a saltspoonful of pepper, mixed well together. When they have become thoroughly warmed turn into a dish, and serve immediately.

APPLES AND ONIONS—Select sour apples, pare, core and thinly slice. Slice about half as many onions, put some bacon fat in the bottom of a frying-pan and when melted add the apples and onions. Cover the pan and cook until tender, cooking rather slowly. Sprinkle with sugar, and serve with roast pork.

BACON AND SPINACH—Line a pudding dish with thin slices of raw bacon. Take boiled spinach, ready for the table, season with butter, salt and pepper. Take also some boiled carrots, turnips and onions. Whip up the yolk of an egg with pepper and salt, and stir into the carrots and turnips. Arrange the vegetables alternately in the dish and partially fill with boiling water. Steam for an hour. Turn out on a flat dish, and serve with a rich brown gravy.

BOILED CELERY—Trim off the tops of the celery about one-third of their length, and also trim the roots into rounding shape. Save the tops for making cream of celery and for garnishes, cook the celery in salted water until tender, drain, lay on toast, and pour a cream sauce over.

BOSTON BAKED BEANS—Pick over a quart of small pea beans, wash thoroughly and soak over night in warm water. In the morning parboil them until the skins crack open. Pour off the water. Put into the bottom of a glazed earthenware pot, made expressly for the purpose, a pint of hot water in which have been dissolved a half tablespoonful salt, two tablespoonfuls molasses, a half teaspoonful mustard, and a pinch of soda. Pack in the beans until about a third full, then place in it a pound (or less, if preferred) of streaked pig pork, the skin of which has been scored. Cover with a layer of beans, letting the rind of the pork just show through. Now add enough more seasoned hot water to cover the beans, and bake covered in a slow oven all day or night. When done the beans should be soft, tender and moist, but brown and whole, and the pork cooked to a jelly.

BREADED POTATO BALLS—Pare, boil and mash potatoes and whip into three cups of potato three level tablespoons of butter, two tablespoons of hot milk, salt and pepper to taste; also two teaspoons of onion juice and two level tablespoons of chopped parsley, one-quarter cup of grated mild cheese and two well-beaten eggs. Beat well and set aside to cool. Mold into small balls, roll each in beaten egg, in fine stale breadcrumbs, and then fry in deep hot fat.

CABBAGE AND CHEESE—Boil the cabbage in two waters, then drain, cool and chop. Season well with salt and pepper and spread a layer in a buttered baking dish. Pour over this a white sauce made from a tablespoonful each of flour and butter and a cup of milk. Add two or three tablespoonfuls of finely broken cheese. Now add another layer of cabbage, then more of the white sauce and cheese, and so on until all the material is used. Sprinkle with fine crumbs, bake covered about half an hour, then uncover and brown.

CAULIFLOWER AU GRATIN—Select a firm, well-shaped cauliflower, and after the preliminary soaking in cold salt water throw into a kettle of boiling water and cook half an hour, until tender. Drain, pick off the flowers and lay to one side, while you pick the stalks into small pieces. Lay on the bottom of a rather shallow buttered baking dish, sprinkle with pepper, grated cheese and cracker crumbs. Dot with pieces of butter. Add a little milk, then a layer of the flowerets and another sprinkling of milk, cheese and pepper.

CAULIFLOWER FRITTERS—Soak and boil the cauliflower in the usual way, then separate into flowers. Dip each piece into a thin batter, plunge into boiling fat and fry a delicate brown. Serve very hot on napkins. If preferred, the pieces may be dipped into a mixture of salt, pepper, vinegar and oil, then fried.

CREAMED SPAGHETTI—Have two quarts of water boiling in a kettle and one-third of a pound of spaghetti. Hold a few pieces of the spaghetti at a time in the water and as the ends soften turn them round and round and down into the kettle. When all are in the water put on a cover and cook the spaghetti twenty minutes, then drain.

Make a cream sauce with a rounding tablespoon each of flour and butter and one cup of cream. Season with one-half teaspoon of salt and a few grains of pepper. Stir in the spaghetti cut in inch pieces, turn on to a dish, and sprinkle with finely grated cheese.

FRIED CORN—Cut the corn off the cob, leaving the grains as separate as possible. Fry in just enough butter to keep it from sticking to the pan, stirring very often. When nicely browned add salt and pepper and a little rich cream. Do not set near the fire after adding the cream.

FRIED TOMATOES—Wipe some smooth solid tomatoes and slice and fry in a spider with butter or pork fat. Season well with salt and pepper.

GLAZED CARROTS WITH PEAS—Wash, scrape and cut three medium-sized carrots in one-fourth inch slices, then in cubes or fancy shapes, drain and put in saucepan with one-half cup butter, one-third cup sugar, and one tablespoon fine chopped fresh mint leaves. Cook slowly until glazed and tender. Drain and rinse one can French peas and heat in freshly boiling water five minutes. Again drain and season with butter, salt and pepper. Mound peas on hot dish and surround with carrots.

GLAZED SWEET POTATOES—Put two rounding table-spoons of butter and one of sugar into a casserole and set on the back of the range to heat slowly. When hot lay in raw, pared sweet potatoes cut in halves, lengthwise. Dust with salt and pepper and put in another layer of seasoned potatoes and enough boiling water to stand one-half inch deep in the dish. Put on the closefitting cover and set in the oven to cook slowly. When the potatoes are tender serve in the same dish with the sweet sauce that will not be entirely absorbed in the cooking. This way of preparing sweet potatoes pleases the Southern taste, which demands sugar added to the naturally sweet vegetable.

GLAZED SWEET POTATOES—Sweet potatoes, like squash and peas, lose a little of their sweetness in cooking, and when recooked it is well to add a little sugar. Slice two large cooked sweet potatoes and lay in a small baking dish, sprinkle with a level tablespoon of sugar and a few dashes of salt and pepper, add also some bits of butter. Pour in one-half cup of boiling water, bake half an hour, basting twice with the butter and water.

GREEN MELON SAUTE—There are frequently a few melons left on the vines which will not ripen sufficiently to be palatable uncooked. Cut them in halves, remove the seeds and then cut in slices three-fourths of an inch thick. Cut each slice in quarters and again, if the melon is large, pare off the rind, sprinkle them slightly with salt and powdered sugar, cover with fine crumbs, then dip in beaten egg, then in crumbs again, and cook slowly in hot butter, the same as eggplant. Drain, and serve hot. When the melons are nearly ripe they may be sauted in butter without crumbs.

JAPANESE OR CHINESE RICE—Wash one cup of rice, rubbing it through several waters until the water runs clear. Put in porcelain-lined stewpan with a quart of soup stock and bay leaves and boil twenty minutes. The stock must be hot when added to the rice. Shake the kettle in which it is cooking several times during the cooking and lift occasionally with a fork. Do not stir. Pour off any superfluous stock remaining at the end of twenty minutes, and set on the back of the stove or in the oven, uncovered, to finish swelling and steaming. Just before serving add one cup of hot tomato juice, a quarter cup of butter, a tablespoon chopped parsley, a dash of paprika, and one tablespoon of grated cheese. Serve with grated cheese.

LIMA BEANS WITH NUTS—Soak one cup of dry lima beans over night. In the morning rip off the skins, rinse and put into the bean pot with plenty of water and salt to season, rather more than without the nuts. Let cook slowly in the oven and until perfectly tender; add one-half cup of walnut meal, stirring it in well; let cook a few minutes, and serve.

MACARONI WITH APRICOTS—Stew twenty halves of fresh apricots in half a cup of sugar and enough water to make a nice sirup when they are done. Before removing from the fire add a heaping tablespoonful of brown flour and cook until the sirup is heavy and smooth. Parboil ten sticks of macaroni broken in two-inch pieces, drain, add to one pint of scalding hot milk two ounces of sugar. Throw in the parboiled. macaroni and allow it to simmer until the milk is absorbed; stir it often. Pour all the juice or sauce from the apricots into the macaroni, cover the macaroni well, set on back of the stove for fifteen minutes, then take off and allow to cool. When cold form a pile of macaroni in the center of the dish and cover with apricots, placing them in circles around and over it.

MACARONI AND CHEESE—Cook macaroni broken up into short length in boiling salted water. Boil uncovered for twenty or thirty minutes, then drain. Fill a buttered pudding dish with alternate layers of macaroni and grated cheese, sprinkling pepper, salt and melted butter over each layer. Have top layer of cheese, moisten with rich milk, bake in moderate oven until a rich brown.

SCRAMBLED CAULIFLOWER—Trim off the coarse outer leaves of a cauliflower. After soaking and cooking, drain well and divide into branches. Sprinkle with nutmeg, salt and pepper and toss into a frying pan with hot butter or olive oil.

MACARONI OR SPAGHETTI SERVED IN ITALIAN STYLE—Break a pound of macaroni or spaghetti into small pieces. Put into boiling salted water and boil about twenty minutes. Then drain and arrange on platter. Sprinkle on each layer grated cheese and mushroom sauce. Serve hot.

MUSHROOM SAUCE, ITALIAN STYLE—(For macaroni, spaghetti, ravioli and rice.)—A small piece of butter about the size of an egg. One or two small onions, cut very small. About two pounds of beef. Let all brown. Prepare as you would a pot roast. Add Italian dried mushrooms, soaked over night in hot water, chopped in small pieces. Add about one-half can of tomatoes. Let all cook well. Salt and pepper to taste. Add a little flour to thicken.

MOLD SPINACH—Remove roots and decayed leaves, wash in several waters until no grit remains. Boil in water to nearly cover until tender, drain, rinse in cold water, drain again, chop very fine, reheat in butter, season with salt and pepper and pack in small cups. Turn out and garnish with sifted yolk of egg.

NUT PARSNIP STEW—Wash, scrape and slice thin two good-sized parsnips. Cook until perfectly tender in two quarts of water. When nearly done add a teaspoon of salt and when thoroughly done a teaspoon of flour mixed with a little cold water, stir well and let boil until the flour is well cooked, then stir in one-half cup of walnut meal, let boil up once, and serve immediately.

POTATOES A LA MAITRE D'HOTEL—Slice cold boiled potatoes thin. Melt a rounding tablespoonful of butter in a saucepan, add a heaping pint bowl of the potatoes, season with salt and pepper, and heat. Now add a teaspoon of lemon juice and the same of finely minced parsley, and serve at once.

POTATOES AU GRATIN—Make a white sauce, using one tablespoonful of butter, one of flour, one-half a teaspoonful salt, one-quarter of a teaspoonful of white pepper and one cupful of milk. Cut cold boiled potatoes into thick slices, or, better still, into half-inch cubes. Butter a baking dish, put in it a layer of the sauce, then one of the potatoes, previously lightly seasoning with salt and pepper. Continue until all are in, the proportion of potato being about two cupfuls.

To one cupful of dried and sifted bread-crumbs, add one teaspoonful of melted butter and stir until it is evenly mixed through. Spread this over the contents of the baking dish, and place in a quick oven for twenty minutes, or until nicely browned. For a change, a little onion juice, chopped parsley or grated cheese may be added to the sauce.

POTATO CREAMED—Cut cold boiled potatoes into small dice and cover them in a small saucepan with milk. Let them stand where they will heat slowly and absorb nearly all the milk. When hot add to one pint of potatoes a tablespoon of salt and a dash of white pepper. Sprinkle a little finely chopped parsley over the top as a garnish.

POTATO MOLD—Mash some potato smoothly, add to it some butter and a little milk to make it smooth but not wet. Season with white pepper and salt and add enough chopped parsley to make it look pretty. Press into greased mold and bake for half an hour until lightly browned. Dust with crumbs and serve.

POTATO PARISIENNE—Potato marbles seasoned with minced parsley, butter and lemon juice are liked by many. Oth-ers find that they are not sufficiently seasoned, that is, the season-ing has not penetrated into the potatoes, especially if a large cut-ter has been used. This method will be found to rem-edy this fault, giving a seasoning which reaches every portion of the po-tato. It may not be quite so attractive as the some-what underdone marbles, but the flavor is finer.

Pare the potatoes and steam or boil them until soft, being careful they do not cook too fast. Drain off the water and let them stand uncovered until dry. Then cut in quarters length-wise, and then in thin slices, letting them drop into a stew-pan containing melted butter, salt and paprika. When all are sliced cover them and let them heat for a few minutes, add minced parsley and lemon juice, shake them about so the seasoning will be well mixed and serve at once.

POTATO PUFFS—No. 1—To one cup of mashed potato add one tablespoon of butter, one egg, beaten light, one-half cup of cream or milk, a little salt. Beat well and fill popover pans half full. Bake until brown in quick oven.

POTATO PUFFS—No. 2—Add hot milk to cold mashed po-tato beat up thoroughly. Add one or two well-beaten eggs, leav-ing out the yolks if preferred whiter. Drop in spoonfuls on a buttered tin, place a piece of butter on the top of each and bake a delicate brown or put in a pudding dish and butter the top and bake till of a light brown on top. Fifteen minutes in a hot oven will be sufficient.

RICE A LA GEORGIENNE FOR FIVE PERSONS—Wash one pound of rice in several changes of cold water until water is clear, and cook until soft, but not soft enough to mash between the fingers. Let it drip, cool and drip again. Add it to one-quarter pound of melted butter, not browned, season with salt and pepper. Mix thoroughly; bake in covered dish for twenty minutes.

RICE IN TOMATOES—Cook some rice in boiling salted water until tender and season highly with pepper. Cut a small slice from the top of each ripe tomato, take out the seeds, fill with the seasoned rice, put a bit of butter on each, set in the oven and bake until the tomato is tender.

RICE SERVED IN ITALIAN STYLE WITH MUSH-ROOM SAUCE—Steam or boil one-half pound of rice until done, then drain. Remove meat from mushroom sauce. Drop rice into mushroom sauce and cook about five minutes. Pour on platter and sprinkle heavy with grated cheese.

SCALLOPED TOMATOES—Drain a half can of tomatoes from some of their liquor and season with salt, pepper, a few drops of onion juice and one teaspoonful sugar. Cover the bottom of a small buttered baking dish with buttered cracker crumbs, cover with tomatoes and sprinkle the top thickly with buttered crumbs. Bake in a hot oven. Buttered cracker crumbs are made by simply rolling common crackers with a rolling pin and allowing one-third cupful of melted butter to each cupful of crumbs. This recipe takes about one and one-third cupfuls of crumbs.

SPAGHETTI A L'ITALIENNE—Let it cook until the water nearly boils away and it is very soft. The imported spaghetti is so firm that it may be cooked a long time without losing its shape. When the water has boiled out, watch it and remove the cover so it will dry off. Then draw the mass to one side and put in a large lump of butter, perhaps a tablespoon, and let it melt, then stir in until the butter is absorbed, and pour on one cup of the strained juice from canned tomatoes. Season with salt and paprika and let it stew until the spaghetti has absorbed the tomato. The spaghetti, if cooked until soft, will thicken the tomato sufficiently and it is less work than to make a tomato sauce. Turn out and serve as an entree, or a main dish for luncheon and pass grated sap sago or other cheese to those who prefer it. When you have any stock like chicken or veal, add that with the tomato or alone if you prefer and scant the butter.

STUFFED CABBAGE—Cut the stalk out of two or more young cabbages and fill with a stuffing made from cooked veal, chopped or ground very fine, seasoned well with salt and pepper, and mixed with the beaten yolk of an egg. Tie a strip of cheese cloth round each cabbage, or if small, twine will hold each together. Put into a kettle with boiling water to cover and cook until tender. Drain, unbind and serve hot.

STUFFED EGG PLANT—Wash a large egg plant, cut in halves the long way and scoop the inside out with a teaspoon, leaving each shell quite empty, but unbroken. Cook the inside portion in one-half cup of water, then press through a strainer and mix with one-half cup of bread crumbs, one rounding tablespoon of butter and season with salt and pepper. The shells should lie in salt and water after scraping, and when ready to fill them wipe them dry and pack the filling. Scatter fine crumbs over the top, dot with butter and bake twenty minutes.

STUFFED POTATOES—Select smooth, even sized potatoes and bake until done. Remove one end, carefully scrape out the center of each mash and season with salt and butter, add a generous portion of nut meat and fill the shells with the mixture. Cover with the piece that was cut off, wrap each potato in tissue paper and serve.

CORN STEWED WITH CREAM—Select a half dozen ears of Indian corn, remove the silks and outer husks, place them in a saucepan and cover with water. Cook, drain, and cut the corn off the cobs with a sharp knife, being careful that none of the cob adheres to the corn. Place in a stew-pan with one cup of hot bechamel sauce, one-half breakfast-cupful of cream and about one-quarter of an ounce of butter. Season with pepper and salt and a little grated nutmeg. Cook gently on a stove for five minutes, place in a hot dish and serve.

SAUCES

CUCUMBER SAUCE—Pare two good sized cucumbers and cut a generous piece from the stem end. Grate on a coarse grater and drain through cheese cloth for half an hour. Season the pulp with salt, pepper and vinegar to suit the taste. Serve with broiled, baked or fried fish.

GHERKIN SAUCE—Put a sprig of thyme, a bay-leaf, a clove of garlic, two finely chopped shallots, and a cayenne pepper, and salt into a saucepan, with one breakfast cup of vinegar. Place pan on fire and when contents have boiled for thirty minutes, add a breakfast cup of stock or good broth. Strain it through a fine hair sieve and stir in one and one-half ounces of liquefied butter mixed with a little flour to thicken it. Place it back in the saucepan and when it boils stir in it a teaspoonful or so of parsley very finely chopped, two or three ounces of pickle gherkins, and a little salt if required.

GIBLET SAUCE—Put the giblets from any bird in the saucepan with sufficient stock or water to cover them and boil for three hours, adding an onion and a few pepper-corns while cooking. Take them out, and when they are quite tender strain the liquor into another pan and chop up the gizzards, livers, and other parts into small pieces. Take a little of the thickening left at the bottom of the pan in which a chicken or goose has been braised, and after the fat has been taken off, mix it with the giblet liquor and boil until dissolved. Strain the sauce, put in the pieces of giblet, and serve hot.

GOOSEBERRY SAUCE—Pick one pound of green gooseberries and put them into a saucepan with sufficient water to keep them from burning, when soft mash them, grate in a little nutmeg and sweeten to taste with moist sugar. This sauce may be served with roast pork or goose instead of apple sauce. It may also be served with boiled mackerel. A small piece of butter will make the sauce richer.

74

"Marvellous [sic] sauce." Photograph by Jehan Georges Vibert (1840-1902).

Courtesy of the Library of Congress.

EDW. NEUMANN, BROADWAY MARKET, DETROIT, MI, BETWEEN 1905 AND 1915.

Photograph courtesy of the Library of Congress.

HALF-GLAZE SAUCE—Put one pint of clear concentrated veal gravy in a saucepan, mix it with two wine-glassfuls of Madeira, a bunch of sweet herbs, and set both over the fire until boiling. Mix two tablespoonfuls of potato flour to a smooth paste with a little cold water, then mix it with the broth and stir until thick. Move the pan to the side of the fire and let the sauce boil gently until reduced to two-thirds of its original quantity. Skim it well, pass it through a silk sieve, and it is ready for use.

HAM SAUCE—After a ham is nearly all used up pick the small quantity of meat still remaining, from the bone, scrape away the uneatable parts and trim off any rusty bits from the meat, chop the bone very small and beat the meat almost to a paste. Put the broken bones and meat together into a saucepan over a slow fire, pour over them one-quarter pint of broth, and stir about one-quarter of an hour, add to it a few sweet herbs, a seasoning of pepper and one-half pint of good beef stock. Cover the saucepan and stir very gently until well flavored with herbs, then strain it. A little of this added to any gravy is an improvement.

HORSERADISH SAUCE—Place in a basin one tablespoonful of moist sugar, one tablespoonful of ground mustard, one teacupful of grated horseradish, and one teaspoonful of turmeric, season with pepper and salt and mix the ingredients with a teacupful of vinegar or olive oil. When quite smooth, turn the sauce into a sauceboat, and it is ready to be served.

LEMON BUTTER—Cream four level tablespoons of butter and add gradually one tablespoon of lemon juice mixing thoroughly.

LEMON SAUCE FOR FISH—Squeeze and strain the juice of a large lemon into a lined saucepan, put in with it one-fourth pound butter and pepper, and salt to taste. Beat it over the fire until thick and hot, but do not allow to boil. When done mix with sauce the beaten yolks of two eggs. It is then ready to be served.

LOBSTER BUTTER—Take the head and spawn of some hen lobsters, put them in a mortar and pound, add an equal quantity of fresh butter, and pound both together, being sure they are thoroughly mixed. Pass this through a fine hair sieve, and the butter is then ready for use. It is very nice for garnishing or for making sandwiches.

MAITRE D'HOTEL BUTTER—Cream one-fourth cup of butter. Add one-half teaspoon salt, a dash of pepper and a tablespoon of fine chopped parsley, then, very slowly to avoid curd-ling, a tablespoon of lemon juice. This sauce is appropriate for beefsteak and boiled fish.

SAUCE A LA METCALF—Put two or three tablespoonfuls of butter in a saucepan, and when it melts add about a tablespoonful of Liebig's Extract of Beef; season and gradually stir in about a cupful of cream. After taking off, add a wine-glassful of Sherry or Madeira.

PARSLEY AND LEMON SAUCE—Squeeze the juice from a lemon, remove the pips, and mince fine the pulp and rind. Wash a good handful of parsley, and shake it as dry as possible, and chop it, throwing away the stalks. Put one ounce of butter and one tablespoonful of flour into a saucepan, and stir over fire until well mixed. Then put in the parsley and minced lemon, and pour in as much clear stock as will be required to make the sauce. Season with a small quantity of pounded mace, and stir the whole over the fire a few minutes. Beat the yolks of two eggs with two tablespoonfuls of cold stock, and move the sauce to the side of the fire, and when it has cooled a little, stir in the eggs. Stir the sauce for two minutes on the side of the fire, and it will be ready for serving.

POIVRADE SAUCE—Put in a stew-pan six scallions, a little thyme, a good bunch of parsley, two bay-leaves, a dessert-spoonful of white pepper, two tablespoonfuls of vinegar and two ounces of butter, and let all stew together until nearly all the liquor has evaporated; add one teacupful of stock, two teacupfuls of Spanish sauce. Boil this until reduced to one-half, then serve.

ROYAL SAUCE—Put four ounces of fresh butter and the yolks of two fresh eggs into a saucepan and stir them over the fire until the yolks begin to thicken, but do not allow them to cook hard. Take sauce off the fire and stir in by degrees two tablespoonfuls of tarragon vinegar, two tablespoons of Indian soy, one finely chopped green gherkin, one small pinch of cayenne pepper, and a small quantity of salt. When well incorporated keep sauce in a cold place. When cold serve with fish.

SAUCE FOR FISH—Simmer two cups of milk with a slice of onion, a slice of carrot cut in bits, a sprig of parsley and a bit of bay-leaf for a few minutes. Strain onto one-quarter cup of butter rubbed smooth with the same flour. Cook five minutes and season with a level teaspoon of salt and a saltspoon of pepper.

SAUCE MAYONNAISE—Place in an earthen bowl a couple of fresh egg yolks and one-half teaspoonful of ground English mustard, half pinch of salt, one-half saltspoonful red pepper, and stir well for about three minutes without stopping, then pour in, one drop at a time, one and one-half cupfuls of best olive oil, and should it become too thick, add a little at a time some good vine-gar, stirring constantly.

SAUCE TARTARE—Use one-half level teaspoon of salt and mustard, one teaspoon of powdered sugar, and a few grains of cayenne beaten vigorously with the yolks of two eggs. Add one-half cup of olive oil slowly and dilute as needed with one and one-half tablespoon of vinegar. Add one-quarter cup of chopped pickles, capers and olives mixed.

TARTAR SAUCE—Mix one tablespoon of vinegar, one teaspoon of lemon juice, a saltspoon of salt, a tablespoon of any good catsup and heat over water. Heat one-third cup of butter in a small saucepan until it begins to brown, then strain onto the other ingredients and pour over the fish on the platter.

SHRIMP SAUCE—Pour one pint of poivrade sauce and butter sauce into a saucepan and boil until somewhat reduced. Thicken the sauce with two ounces of lobster butter. Pick one and one-half pints of shrimps, put them into the sauce with a small quantity of lemon juice, stir the sauce by the side of the fire for a few minutes, then serve it.

SAUCE FOR FRIED PIKE—Peel and chop very fine one small onion, one green pepper, half a peeled clove, and garlic. Season with salt, red pepper and half a wineglassful of good white wine. Boil about two minutes and add a gill of tomato sauce and a small tomato cut in dice shaped pieces. Cook about ten minutes.

ROLLS, BREAD AND MUFFINS

BREAKFAST ROLLS—Sift a quart of flour and stir into it a saltspoonful of sugar, a cup of warm milk, two tablespoonfuls of melted shortening and two beaten eggs. Dissolve a quarter of a cake of compressed yeast in a little warm milk and beat in last of all. Set the dough in a bowl to rise until morning. Early in the morning make lightly and quickly into rolls and set to rise near the range for twenty minutes.

EGG ROLLS—Two cups flour, one level teaspoon salt, two level teaspoons baking powder, two level tablespoons lard, two level tablespoons butter, one egg, one-half cup milk. Sift together the flour, salt, and baking powder, work in the shortening with the fingers.

Add the egg well beaten and mixed with the milk. Mix well, toss onto a floured board and knead lightly. Roll out and cut in two-inch squares. Place a half-inch apart in a buttered pan. Gash the center of each with a sharp knife. Brush over with sugar and water, and bake fifteen minutes in a hot oven.

EXCELLENT TEA ROLLS—Scald one cup of milk and turn into the mixing bowl. When nearly cool add a whole yeast cake and beat in one and a half cups of flour. Cover and let rise. Add one-quarter cup of sugar, one level teaspoon of salt, two beaten eggs, and one-third cup of butter. Add flour enough to make a dough that can be kneaded. Cover and let rise. Roll out one-half inch thick, cut in rounds, brush one-heal each with melted butter, fold and press together. Set close together in the pan, cover with a cloth, let rise, and bake.

LIGHT LUNCHEON ROLLS—Heat one cup of milk to the scalding point in a double boiler, add one rounding tablespoon of butter, one level tablespoon of sugar, and one level teaspoon of salt. Stir and set into cold water until lukewarm, then add one yeast cake dissolved in one-quarter cup of lukewarm water, and two cups of flour. Beat hard for two or three minutes, cover,

CALUMET BREAD
CALUMET BISCUITS

HOME-MADE BISCUITS AND BREAD FROM *Reliable Recipes and Helpful Hints,* A CALUMET ADVERTISING COOKBOOK OF 1921.

Two kinds of bread are advertised on boxes outside the A.J. Barnsback Market, Chicago.

Photograph courtesy of the Chicago Public Library

and let rise until very light. Add flour to make a dough that can be kneaded and let rise again. Knead, shape into small rolls. Set them close together in a buttered baking pan, let rise light, and bake in a quick oven.

A PAN OF ROLLS—Scald one pint of milk and add one rounding tablespoon of lard. Mix in one quart of sifted bread flour, one-quarter cup of sugar, a saltspoon of salt and one-half yeast cake dissolved in one-half cup of lukewarm water. Cover and let rise over night. In the morning roll half an inch thick cut into rounds, spread a little soft butter on one-half of each, fold over and press together. Let rise until light and bake in a quick oven. Rolls may be raised lighter than a loaf of bread because the rising is checked as soon as they are put into the oven.

RAISED GRAHAM ROLLS—Scald two cups of milk and melt in it two level tablespoons of butter and one-half level teaspoon of salt. When cool add two tablespoons of molasses and one-half yeast cake dissolved in a little warm water. Add white flour to make a thin batter, beat until smooth and set in a warm place until light. When well risen stir in whole meal to make a dough just stiff enough to knead. Knead until elastic then place it in the original bulk. Flour the board and turn the risen dough out carefully, pat out one inch thick with the rolling pin and make into small rolls. Place these rolls close together in the pan, brush over with milk and let rise until very light. Bake in a quick oven.

RYE BREAKFAST CAKES—Beat the egg light, add one-half cup of sugar, two cups of milk, a saltspoon of salt, one and one-half cups of rye meal, one and one-half cups of flour and three level teaspoons of baking powder. Bake in a hot greased gem pan.

BREAKFAST CAKES—Sift one cup of corn meal, one-quarter teaspoon of salt and two level teaspoons of sugar together, stir in one cup of thick sour milk, one-half tablespoonful melted butter, one well beaten egg and one-half teaspoon of soda, measured level. Beat hard and bake in gem pans in a quick oven.

SCOTCH OAT CAKES—Can be either fried on a griddle or broiled over a fire. The meal for this purpose should be ground fine. Put a quart of the meal in a baking dish with a teaspoonful of salt. Pour in little by little just enough cold water to make a dough and roll out quickly before it hardens into a circular sheet about a quarter of an inch thick. Cut into four cakes and bake slowly for about twenty minutes on an iron griddle. Do not turn but toast after they are cooked.

SCOTCH SCONES—Two cups flour, four level teaspoons baking powder, two level tablespoons sugar, one level teaspoon salt, three level tablespoons butter, one whole egg or two yolks, one cup buttermilk. Sift together the flour, baking powder, sugar and salt, and work in the butter with the fingers, then add the buttermilk and egg well beaten. Mix well, turn onto floured board and knead slightly. Roll out one-half inch thick. Cut with small biscuit cutter and cook on a hot griddle, turning once.

LOG CABIN TOAST FOR BREAKFAST—This is made up of long strips of bread cut to the thinness of afternoon tea sandwiches, then toasted a delicate brown. All are lightly buttered and piled on a hot plate log cabin fashion.

OLD FASHION RUSKS—At night make a sponge as for bread with two cups of scalded milk, a teaspoon of salt, yeast and flour. In the morning put half a cup of butter into two cups of milk and heat until the butter is barely melted, add this to the sponge, one cup of sugar and three beaten eggs. Add flour to make a dough that can be kneaded. Let rise very light. Roll out one and one-half inches thick, cut in round cakes, let rise and bake a deep yellow color.

WAFFLES SOUTHERN STYLE—One pint of flour, one pint buttermilk, one egg, half teaspoon soda dissolved in little water, one teaspoon sugar, one teaspoon salt, one teaspoon baking powder, one tablespoon cornmeal, one tablespoon melted but-ter. Mix as any other batter cake or waffles.

WHOLE WHEAT POPOVERS—Put two-thirds cup of whole wheat meal, one and two-thirds cup of white flour, and one-half level teaspoon of salt into a sifter and sift three times. Pour two cups of milk on slowly and stir until smooth. Beat two eggs five minutes, add to the first mixture, and beat again for two minutes. Turn into hot greased iron gem pans and bake half an hour in a rather quick oven.

BERRY MUFFINS—Mix two cups sifted flour, one-half teaspoon salt and two rounded teaspoons baking powder. Cream one-quarter cup of butter with one-half cup sugar, add well beaten yolk of one egg, one cup milk, the flour mixture and white of egg beaten stiff. Stir in carefully one heaped cup blueberries which have been picked over, rinsed, dried and rolled in flour. Bake in muffin pans twenty minutes.

BUTTERMILK MUFFINS—Sift four cups of flour, one-quarter cup of cornmeal, and one level teaspoon each of salt and soda three times. Beat two eggs well, add a level tablespoon of sugar, four cups of buttermilk, the dry ingredients, and beat hard for two minutes. Bake in muffin rings or hot greased gem pans. One-half the recipe will be enough for a small family.

ENGLISH MUFFINS—One pint milk, two level tablespoons shortening (butter or lard), two level teaspoons sugar, one level teaspoon salt, one yeast cake dissolved in one-fourth cup luke-warm water, flour. Scald the milk and add the shortening, sugar, and salt. When lukewarm add the yeast and sufficient flour to make a good batter. Here one's judgment must be used. Beat well and let rise until double in bulk. Warm and butter a griddle and place on it buttered muffin rings. Fill not quite half full of the batter, cover and cook slowly until double, then heat the griddle quickly and cook for about ten minutes, browning nicely underneath. Then turn them and brown the other side. When cool split, toast and butter.

GRAHAM MUFFINS—Heat to the boiling point two cups of milk, add a tablespoon of butter and stir until melted. Sift two cups of whole wheat flour, one-half cup of white flour, two teaspoons of baking powder. Pour on the milk and butter, beat, add the yolks of two eggs well beaten, then the stiffly beaten whites. Bake in hot greased gem pans.

HOMINY MUFFINS—Sift twice together one and one-half cups of flour, three level teaspoons of baking powder, one level tablespoon of sugar, and a saltspoon of salt. To one cup of boiled hominy add two tablespoons of melted butter and one cup of milk. Add to the dry ingredients and beat, then add two well beaten eggs. Pour the batter into hot greased gem pans and bake.

MUFFINS—Sift a saltspoon of salt, two level teaspoons of baking powder, and two cups of flour together. Beat the yolks of two eggs, add one clip of milk, two tablespoons of melted butter, and the dry ingredients. Beat, add lightly the stiffly beaten whites of two eggs, fill hot buttered gem pans two-thirds full, and bake in a hot oven.

QUICK MUFFINS IN RINGS—Beat two eggs, yolks and whites separately. Add to the yolks two cups of milk, one level teaspoon of salt, one tablespoon of melted butter and two cups of flour in which two level teaspoons of baking powder have been sifted, and last the stiffly beaten whites of the eggs. When well mixed bake in greased muffin rings on a hot griddle. Turn over when risen and set, as both sides must be browned.

BOILED RICE MUFFINS—To make muffins with cooked rice, sift two and one-quarter cups of flour twice with five level teaspoons of baking powder, one rounding tablespoon of sugar, and a saltspoon of salt. Put in one well beaten egg, half a cup of milk, and three-quarters cup of boiled rice mixed with another half cup of milk, and two tablespoons of melted butter. Beat well, pour into hot gem pans and bake.

BOSTON BROWN BREAD—To make one loaf sift together one cup of cornmeal, one cup rye meal, and one cup of graham flour, with three-quarters cup of molasses and one and three-quarters cup sweet milk. Add one-half teaspoonful of soda dissolved in warm water. Turn into a well buttered mold which may be a five-pound lard pail, if no other mold is handy. Set on something that will keep mold from bottom of kettle and turn enough boiling water to come half way up on the mold. Cover the kettle and keep the kettle boiling steadily for three and one-half hours. If water boils away add enough boiling water to keep the same amount of water in kettle. Put in molds and cut when cool.

CRISP WHITE CORNCAKE—Two cups scalded milk, one cup white cornmeal, two level teaspoons salt. Mix the salt and cornmeal and add gradually the hot milk. When well mixed, pour into a buttered dripping pan and bake in a moderate oven until crisp. Serve cut in squares. The mixture should not be more than one-fourth inch deep when poured into pan.

CROUTONS—Croutons made coarsely are no addition to a soup. For the best sort, cut out stale bread into half-inch slices, spread with butter, then trim away the crust. Cut into small cubes, put into a pan and set in a hot oven. If the croutons incline to brown unevenly shake the pan.

EGG BREAD—One pint of boiling water, half pint white cornmeal to teaspoon salt, two tablespoonfuls of butter, two eggs, one cup milk, bake in a moderate oven.

GRAHAM BREAD—Put one cup of scalded and cooled milk, one cup of water, two cups of flour and one-half yeast cake dissolved in one cup of lukewarm water into a bowl and let rise over night. In the morning add a level teaspoon of salt, two rounding cups of graham flour and one-half cup sugar. Beat well, put into two pans and let rise until light and bake one hour.

NUT BREAD—One and one-half cups of white flour, two cups of graham flour, one-half cup of cornmeal, one-half cup of brown sugar and molasses, one pint of sweet milk, one cup of chopped walnuts, two teaspoons of baking powder, one-half teaspoon of salt. Bake in a long pan for three-quarters of an hour.

OATMEAL BREAD—Over a pint of rolled oats pour a quart of boiling water. When cool add one teaspoonful suet, one teaspoon butter, one-half cup molasses and one-half yeast cake dissolved in a little water. Stir this thoroughly and then add two quarts sifted flour. Do not knead this and allow it to rise over night, and in the morning stir it again, and then put it in well buttered bread pans: let it rise until it fills the pans and then bake in a moderate oven. It takes a little longer to bake than white bread.

OATMEAL BREAD—Cook one cup of rolled oats in water for serving at breakfast, and one cup of molasses, one and one-half cups of lukewarm water in which is dissolved one yeast cake and one teaspoon of salt. Mix in enough flour to make a stiff dough, cover and let rise. When very light stir down, put in pans, let rise light and bake in a slow oven. The heat should be sufficient at first to check the rising, then the baking should be slow.

ORIENTAL OATMEAL BREAD—Take two cupfuls of rolled oats, put in bread pan, turn on four cupfuls of boiling water, stir for awhile. Add, while hot, a heaping tablespoonful of lard or one scant tablespoonful of butter and one of lard, two teaspoonfuls of salt and four tablespoonfuls of sugar and three of molasses. Now add two cupfuls of cold water (making six cups of water in all) and, if cool enough, add one yeast cake dissolved in a very little water. Now stir in all the white flour it will take until it is as stiff as you can manage it with the spoon. Set in warm place over night, and in the morning with spoon and knife fill your tins part full, let rise to nearly top of pan, then bake an hour for medium size loaves.

RAISIN BREAD—Scald three cups of milk and add one teaspoon of salt and two tablespoons of sugar. Cool and add one-half yeast cake, dissolved in one-quarter cup of lukewarm water. Mix in enough flour to make a drop batter and set to rise. When this sponge is light put in two cups of seeded raisins and enough flour to make a soft dough, but stiff enough to knead. Let rise again, then mold into two loaves. Let the loaves double in size and bake slowly, covering with another pan for the first twenty minutes of baking.

STEAMED BROWN BREAD—Beat one egg light, add one cup of cornmeal, one cup rye-meal and one and one-half cups of flour sifted with a half level teaspoon of salt. Add one cup of molasses, and after it is turned out put in one level teaspoon of soda and fill with boiling water. Add to the other one-third cup more of the water. Pour into well buttered mold and steam four hours.

SOUTHERN CORNCAKE—Mix two cups of white corn-meal, a rounding tablespoon of sugar and a level teaspoon of salt, then pour enough hot milk or milk and water to moisten the meal well, but not to make it of a soft consistency. Let stand until cool, then add three well beaten eggs and spread on a buttered shallow pan about half an inch thick. Bake in a quick oven cut in squares, split and butter while hot.

STEAMED CORN BREAD—Sift together one cup corn-meal and flour and a level teaspoon of salt. Put one level tea-spoon soda in one tablespoon of water, add to one-half cup of molasses and stir into the meal with one and two-thirds cups of milk. Beat and turn into a greased mold. Steam four hours, take off the lid of the mold and set in the oven fifteen minutes.

STEAMED GRAHAM BREAD—Put into a mixing bowl two cups of sour milk, one cup of molasses, one level teaspoon of salt, two of soda and then enough graham flour to make a batter as stiff as can be stirred with a spoon, adding one-half cup of seeded raisins. Pour into a two-quart mold or lard pail well greased, cover closely and set in a kettle of boiling water that comes two-thirds the depth of the mold. Cover the kettle and keep the water boiling constantly for four hours.

WHOLE WHEAT BREAD—Scald one cupful of milk and one teaspoonful of butter, one of salt, one cup of water and one tablespoonful of sugar. When lukewarm add half a cake of compressed yeast dissolved in a little water and enough wheat flour to make a thin batter. Beat vigorously until smooth and let rise until very light. Add as much whole wheat flour as you can beat in with a spoon. Pour into greased tins, let rise until light and bake in moderate oven for one hour.

ASPARAGUS FRITTERS—Make a thick sauce with one-half cup of milk, one rounding tablespoon of butter and one-quarter cup of flour. Stir in one cup of cooked asparagus tips and cool. Add one beaten egg and cook on a hot buttered griddle in small cakes.

CORN FRITTERS—One-half can corn, one-half cup flour, one-half level teaspoon baking powder, one level teaspoon salt, a dash of cayenne and one egg. Chop the corn fine and add the flour, sifted with the baking powder, salt and cayenne. Add the egg yolk, well beaten and fold in the white beaten stiff. Drop by spoonfuls into hot fat one-half inch deep. Turn once while cooking. When done, drain on brown paper and serve.

CRUMB GRIDDLE CAKES—Soak one pint of bread crumbs in one pint of sour milk for an hour, then add a level teaspoon of soda dissolved in one cup of sweet milk, and one well beaten egg, half a teaspoon of salt and flour enough to make a drop batter as thick as griddle cakes are usually made.

HOMINY CAKES—To two cups of boiled hominy add two tablespoons of melted butter. Break the whole very fine with spoon or fork. Add two well beaten eggs, one-third teaspoon of salt, and a saltspoon of pepper. Form into little cakes, after adding enough milk to make it of the right consistency to handle. Set cakes on buttered dish and dust with a little finely grated cheese. Bake in hot oven and serve at once.

OATMEAL CAKE—Mix fine oatmeal into a stiff dough with milk-warm water, roll it to the thinness almost of a wafer, bake on a griddle or iron plate placed over a slow fire for three or four minutes, then place it on edge before the fire to harden. This will be good for months, if kept in a dry place.

PINEAPPLE PANCAKES—Make a batter using half pound sifted flour and three good sized eggs with a cupful of milk. This makes a very thin batter. When smooth and free from lumps, bake in a well buttered frying pan, making the cakes about eight inches in diameter. As soon as brown on one side turn. When cooked on both sides remove to a hot serving dish and sprinkle with sweetened pineapple. Bake the remainder of batter in the same way, piling in layers with the pineapple between the cakes. Cut in triangular pieces like pie and serve very hot.

SQUASH FRITTERS—To two cups of mashed dry winter squash add one cup of milk, two well beaten eggs, one teaspoon of salt, a little pepper and one heaping teaspoon of baking powder. Beat well and drop by spoonfuls into hot butter or cooking oil and fry.

PIES AND PASTRIES

A GOOD CRUST FOR GREAT PIES—To a peck of flour, add the yolks of three eggs. Boil some water, put in half a pound of fried suet and a pound and a half of butter. Skim off the butter and suet and as much of the liquor as will make a light crust. Mix well and roll out.

CRUST FOR CUSTARDS—Take a half pound of flour, six ounces of butter, the yolks of two eggs, three spoonfuls of cream. Mix well and roll very thin.

DRIPPING CRUST—Take a pound and a half of beef drippings; boil in water, strain and let it get cold, taking off the hard fat. Scrape off and boil it four or five times; then work it up well into three pounds of flour, then add enough cold water to make dough, just stiff enough to roll. This makes a very fine crust.

PASTE FOR TARTS—One pound of flour, three-quarters of a pound of butter and just enough cold water to mix together. Beat well with a rolling pin.

PUFF PASTE—Take a quarter of a peck of flour, rub in a pound of butter, make it up into a light paste with a little cold water, just stiff enough to handle; then roll out to about the thickness of a crown piece. Spread over with butter and sprinkle over with flour, then double up and roll out again. Double and roll out seven or eight times. It is then fit for all kinds of pies and tarts that require a puff paste.

APPLE PIE—Make up a puff paste crust and lay some around the sides of a dish. Pare and quarter apples. Put a layer of apples in the dish, sprinkle with sugar, and add a little lemon peel, cut up fine, a little lemon juice, a few cloves; then the rest of the apples, sugar and so on. Sweeten to taste. Boil the peels and cores of the apples in a little water, strain and boil

CLEVELAND BAKING POWDER PLACED THIS ADVERTISEMENT
IN *The Outlook* OF JANUARY 7, 1899.

Enterprise Cherry Stoners

RECOMMENDED FOR RAPID AND EFFECTIVE WORK

The Nos. 1 and 2 can be adjusted by thumb screws for different sized cherries. The Nos. 17 and 18 are constructed with a new patented regulating device the simplicity of which makes it easier to adjust machine for different sized cherries and absolutely insures the jaws retaining their position when set.

ILLUSTRATION SHOWS DESIGN
NOS. 1, 2, 17 AND 18.

No. 1—Japanned . . . 65c.   No. 17—Japanned . . . 75c.

No. 2—Tinned . . . . 75c.   No. 18—Tinned . . . . 90c.

The No. 12 Stoner is intended to stone cherries with the least possible cutting or disfiguring. Every good housewife will appreciate this for preserving purposes. The most satisfactory results are obtained by dropping the cherries one at a time into the hopper immediately after sweeper has passed the hole. With practice one can become expert.

No. 12   TINNED $1.25

COOKS OF 1906 COULD REMOVE THE STONES FROM CHERRIES WITH AN ENTERPRISE CHERRY STONER, AVAILABLE FOR $1.25 OR LESS.

the syrup with a little sugar. Pour over the apples. Put on the upper crust and bake. A little quince or marmalade may be used, if desired.

Pears may be used instead of apples, omitting the quince or marmalade.

Pies may be buttered when taken from oven. If a sauce is desired, beat up the yolks of two eggs, add half pint of cream, little nutmeg and sugar. Put over a slow fire, stirring well until it just boils up. Take off the upper crust and pour the sauce over the pie, replacing the crust.

APPLE PIE—SOUTHERN STYLE—For four pies half pound butter, quarter pound of lard, half dinner teaspoon of salt, work four cups flour and the above ingredients with a fork, and then mix with ice water and mix it so it will just stick together. Then ready for use.

BEATEN CREAM PIE—Line a plate with good paste, prick in several places to prevent rising out of shape. Bake and spread over some jelly or jam about half an inch thick, and cover with one cup of cream beaten stiff with two rounding tablespoons of powdered sugar and flavored with one teaspoon of vanilla.

LARGE LEMON PIE—Mix three level teaspoons of corn starch smooth in a little cold water, and stir into three cups of boiling water. Cook five minutes; stir in one level tablespoon of butter, the juice and grated yellow rind of two lemons, one and one-half cups of sugar, and the yolks of three eggs. Cook until the egg thickens, take from the fire and cool. Line a large pie plate with paste and gash it in several places to prevent rising unevenly, bake and fill with the mixture. Cover with a meringue made from the white of three eggs beaten with six level tablespoons of powdered sugar. Set in the oven to color.

LEMON PIE—This is an old fashion pie, because it is baked between two crusts, yet many have called it the best of all kinds. Grate the yellow rind of two lemons, take off all the white skin and chop the remainder very fine, discarding all the seeds. Add two cups of sugar and two beaten eggs. Mix well and pour into a paste lined plate cover, and bake thirty minutes.

NUT MINCE PIES—One cup of walnut meats chopped fine, two cups of chopped apple, one cup of raisins, one and one-half cups of sugar mixed with one teaspoon each of cinnamon and allspice and one-half teaspoon each of cloves and salt, one-half cup of vinegar and one-half cup of water or fruit juice. Mix thoroughly. This quantity makes two large pies.

PINEAPPLE CREAM PIE—One-half cup butter, one cup sugar, one can shredded pineapple, one-half cup milk, two eggs. Cream the butter, add gradually the sugar, then the pineapple, milk and eggs well beaten. Mix well and bake in one crust like custard pie. When cool cover with a meringue or with whipped cream sweetened and flavored with vanilla.

PLAIN PIE PASTE—Sift one and one-half cups of flour with a saltspoon of salt and rub in one-quarter cup of lard. Moisten with very cold water until a stiff dough is formed. Pat out and lay on one-quarter cup of cold butter rolled out in a sheet. Fold in three layers, turn half way round, and pat out again. Fold and roll twice more. This will make one large pie with two crusts.

CHERRY PIE—Make a good crust, lining the sides of a pie pan. Place stoned cherries, well sweetened, in the pan and cover with upper crust. Bake in slow oven. (A few red currants may be added to the cherries if desired.)

Plums or gooseberry pies may be made in the same way.

CHERRY PIE—Roll two large soda crackers into fine dust and stone cherries enough to measure two cups. Line a pie plate with good rich paste and scatter one-half cup of sugar over. Sprinkle one-half of the cracker dust, and over that one-half of the cherries. Repeat the three layers, pour on one cup of cherry juice and cold water, cover with paste and bake in a moderate oven.

FRESH RASPBERRY PIE—Line a pie plate with rich paste, fill with raspberries and scatter on sugar to sweeten. Cover with a crust and bake in a quick oven. When done draw from the oven, cut a gash in the top, and pour in the following mixture: The yolks of two eggs beaten light with a tablespoon of sugar and mixed with one cup of hot thin cream. Set back in the oven for five minutes.

GREEN CURRANT PIE—Stew and mash a pint of rather green currants, sweeten abundantly, add a sprinkling of flour or a rolled cracker and bake with two crusts. Dust generously with powdered sugar.

GREEN TOMATO PIE—Take green tomatoes not yet turned and peel and slice wafer thin. Fill a plate nearly full, add a tablespoonful vinegar and plenty of sugar, dot with bits of butter and flavor with nutmeg or lemon. Bake in one or two crusts as preferred.

LEMON CREAM PIE—Stir into one cup of boiling water one tablespoonful of cornstarch dissolved in a little cold water. Cook until thickened and clear, then add one cup of sugar, a teaspoonful of butter, and the juice and grated rind of two lemons. Add the beaten yolks of three eggs and take from the fire. Have ready the bottom crust of a pie that has been baked, first pricking with a fork to prevent blisters. Place the custard in the crust and bake half an hour. When done take from the oven and spread over the top a meringue made from the stiffly whipped whites of the eggs, and three tablespoonfuls of sugar. Shut off the oven so it will be as cool as possible giving the meringue plenty of time to rise, stiffen and color to a delicate gold.

APPLE FRITTERS—Beat the yolks of eight eggs and the white of four together. Add a quart of cream. Put over a fire and heat until you can bear your finger in it. Add quarter of a pint of sack, three-quarters of a pint of ale and make a passet of it. When cool put in nutmeg, ginger, salt and flour. The batter should be pretty thick. Add pippins, sliced or scraped and fry in deep fat.

APPLE SLUMP—Fill a deep baking dish with apples, pared, cored and sliced. Scatter on a little cinnamon and cover with good paste rolled a little thicker than for pie. Bake in a moderate oven until the apples are done, serve in the same dish, cutting the crust into several sections. Before cutting, the crust may be lifted and the apples seasoned with butter and sugar, or the seasoning may be added after serving. A liquid or a hard sauce may be served with the slump. If the apples are a kind that do not cook easily bake half an hour, then put on the crust and set back in the oven.

BREAD PUFFS WITH SAUCE—When bread dough is raised light, cut off small pieces and pull out two or three inches long. Fry like doughnuts in deep fat and put into a deep dish, turn over the puffs a cream sauce seasoned with salt and pepper.

CHERRY DUMPLINGS—Sift two cups of pastry flour with four level teaspoons of baking powder and a saltspoon of salt. Mix with three-quarters cup of milk or enough to make a soft dough. Butter some cups well, put a tablespoon of dough in each, then a large tablespoon of stoned cherries and another tablespoon of dough. Set in a steamer or set the cups in a pan of hot water and into the oven to cook half an hour. Serve with a sweet liquid sauce.

COTTAGE CHEESE TARTLETS—One cup cheese, three level tablespoons sugar, few grains salt, two teaspoons melted butter, one tablespoon lemon juice, yolks two eggs, one-fourth cup milk, whites two eggs. Press the cheese through a potato ricer or sieve, then add the sugar, salt, butter, lemon juice, and the egg yolks well beaten and mixed with the milk. Mix well and fold the whites of the eggs beaten stiff. Line individual tins with pastry and fill three-fourths full with the mixture. Bake in a moderate oven for thirty minutes.

PRUNE TARTS—Wash the prunes thoroughly and soak over night or for several hours. Cook in the same water. When very tender rub them through a sieve. To one cup of the pulp add one tablespoon of lemon juice, the yolks of two eggs beaten with one-half cup of thin cream and a few grains of salt. Mix well and sweeten to taste, then fold in the whites of two eggs beaten very stiff. Line small tins with paste, fill with the mixture and bake in a moderate oven. Serve cold.

RASPBERRY DUMPLINGS—Wash one cup of rice and put into the double boiler. Pour over it two cups of boiling water, add one-half teaspoon of salt and two tablespoons of sugar and cook thirty minutes or until soft. Have some small pudding cloths about twelve inches square, wring them out of hot water and lay them over a small half pint bowl. Spread the rice one-third of an inch thick over the cloth, and fill the center with fresh raspberries. Draw the cloth around until the rice covers the berries and they are a good round shape. Tie the ends of the cloth firmly, drop them into boiling water and cook twenty minutes. Remove the cloth and serve with lemon sauce.

TART SHELLS—Roll out thin a nice puff paste, cut with a small biscuit cutter. With cutter take out the centers of two or three of these, lay the rings thus made on the third and bake immediately. Shells may also be made by lining pattypans with the paste; if the paste is light the shells will be fine and may be used for tarts or oyster patties. Filled with jelly and covered with meringue (a tablespoonful of sugar to the white of an egg), and browned in the oven.

BAVARIAN CREAM—Soak one-quarter of a box of gelatin in cold water until it is soft, then dissolve it in a cup of hot milk with one-third of a cup of sugar. Flavor with vanilla and set away to cool. Whip one pint of cream and when the gelatin is cold and beginning to stiffen stir in the cream lightly. Form in mold.

BOILED CUSTARD—Heat two cups of milk in a double boiler and pour on to the yolks of three eggs beaten light, with three rounding tablespoons of sugar and a pinch of salt. Return to the double boiler and cook until the spoon will coat with the custard. Cool and add flavoring.

CALLA LILIES—Beat three eggs and a rounding cup of sugar together, add two-thirds cup of flour and one-half teaspoon of lemon flavoring. Drop in teaspoonfuls on a buttered sheet, allowing plenty of room to spread in baking. Bake in a moderate oven, take up with a knife, and roll at once into lily shape. Bake but four or five at a time because if the cakes cook even a little they will break. Fill each with a little beaten and sweetened cream.

COCOA CUSTARD—For three cups of milk allow four teaspoons of cocoa, three beaten eggs, three tablespoons of sugar, and three-quarters teaspoon of vanilla. Heat the milk, stir in the cocoa, and cool a little before pouring over the egg and sugar. Bake in custard cups set in a pan of hot water in a moderate oven.

COFFEE CREAM—Have one and one-half cups of strong coffee hot, add one level tablespoon of gelatin soaked in one-half cup of milk for fifteen minutes. When well dissolved add two-thirds cup of sugar, a saltspoon of salt, and the yolks of three eggs beaten light, stir in the double boiler till thick, take from the fire, and add the white of three eggs beaten stiff and one-half teaspoon of vanilla. Fill molds that have been dipped in cold water, set in cool place and when firm unmold and serve with powdered sugar and cream.

COFFEE CUP CUSTARD—One quart milk, one-fourth cup ground coffee, four eggs, one-half cup sugar, one-fourth level teaspoon salt, one-half teaspoon vanilla. Tie the coffee loosely in a piece of cheesecloth and put into double boiler with the milk. Scald until a good coffee color and flavor is obtained, then remove from the fire. Remove the coffee. Beat the eggs and add the sugar, salt and vanilla, then pour on gradually the milk. Strain into cups, place in a pan of hot water, and bake in a moderate oven until firm in the middle. Less vanilla is required when combined with another flavoring.

CAKES, CRULLERS AND E'CLAIRS

ALMOND CAKES—One pound sifted flour, one-half pound butter, three-fourths pound sugar, two eggs, one-half teaspoon ground cinnamon, four ounces of almonds blanched and chopped very fine. Two ounces of raisins finely chopped. Mix all the dry ingredients together, then rub in the butter, add eggs and spices last of all, roll out half an inch thick, cut in fancy shapes and bake in a slow oven.

ALMOND CHEESE CAKES—Blanch and pound to a fine paste one cupful almonds. As you pound them add rose water, a few drops at a time to keep them from oiling. Add the paste to one cupful milk curd, together with a half cup cream, one cupful sugar, three beaten egg yolks and a scant teaspoonful of rose water. Fill patty pans lined with paste and bake in hot oven ten minutes.

AUNT AMY'S CAKE—Take two eggs, one and one-half cups of sugar, one cup of sour milk, one-half cup of butter, two cups of flour and one teaspoonful of soda. Spice to taste. This is a good cake and one which is also inexpensive in baking. Use a moderate oven and bake in loaves rather than sheets.

BALTIMORE CAKE—Beat one cupful of butter to a cream, using a wood cake spoon. Add gradually while beating constantly two cupfuls fine granulated sugar. When creamy add a cupful of milk, alternating with three and one-half cupfuls pastry flour that has been mixed and sifted with two teaspoonfuls of baking powder. Add a teaspoonful of vanilla and the whites of six eggs beaten stiff and dry. Bake in three buttered and floured shallow cake tins, and spread between the layers and on top the following icing: Put in a saucepan three cups sugar, one cup water. Heat gradually to the boiling point, and cook without stirring until the syrup will thread. Pour the hot syrup gradually over the well beaten whites of three eggs and continue beating until of the right consistency for spreading. Then add one cupful chopped and seeded raisins, one cup chopped pecan meats and five figs cut in strips.

CALUMET CHOCOLATE CAKE
CALUMET JELLY LAYER CAKE

CHOCOLATE CAKE AND JELLY LAYER CAKE
FROM *Reliable Recipes and Helpful Hints*, 1921.

MANY OF MR. ESTES RECIPES CALL FOR DATES.
HERE, AN ADVERTISEMENT FOR DROMEDARY DATES
FROM *The Etude*, 1916.

BALTIMORE CAKE—For this cake use one cupful butter, two cupfuls sugar, three and one-half cupfuls flour, one cupful sweet milk, two teaspoonfuls baking powder, the whites of six eggs and a teaspoonful of rose water. Cream the butter, add the sugar gradually, beating steadily, then the milk and flavoring, next the flour sifted with the baking powder, and lastly the stiffly beaten whites folded in at the last. Bake in three layer cake tins in an oven hotter than for loaf cake. While baking prepare the filling. Dissolve three cupfuls sugar in one cupful boiling water, and cook until it spins a thread. Pour over the stiffly beaten whites of three eggs, stirring constantly. Add to this icing one cupful chopped raisins, one cupful chopped nut meats, prefera-bly pecans or walnuts, and a half dozen figs cut in fine strips. Use this for filling and also ice the top and sides with it.

BREAD CAKE—Cream one cup of sugar and one-half cup of butter, add one-half cup of milk, two cups of flour sifted with three teaspoons of baking powder and last the stiffly beaten whites of three eggs and half a teaspoon of vanilla flavoring. Bake in one loaf.

BRIDE'S CAKE—One and one-half cupfuls of sugar, one-half cupful of butter, one-half cupful of sweet milk, two cupfuls of flour, one-quarter cupful cornstarch, six egg whites, one and one-half teaspoonfuls baking powder, one teaspoonful vanilla. Cream the sugar and butter, add milk, flour and cornstarch into which the baking powder has been thoroughly sifted, stir in the whites of eggs quickly with the flavoring.

BUTTERMILK CAKE—Cream three tablespoons of butter with one cup of sugar, add one cup of buttermilk, one well beaten egg, two cups of flour sifted with four teaspoons of baking powder and one-half cup of seeded raisins cut in pieces and rolled in flour.

CHOCOLATE CAKE—Beat one cup of butter to a cream with two cups of sugar, add the yolks of five eggs, beaten until light-colored, and one cup of milk. Sift three and one-half cups of flour with five level teaspoons of baking powder and add to the first mixture. Stir well and fold in the beaten whites of two eggs. Beat in layer cake tins and spread the following mixture between when the cakes are nearly cold. Beat one and one-half cups of powdered sugar, three level tablespoons of cocoa, one teaspoon of vanilla, and the whites of three eggs together until a smooth mixture is made that will spread easily. The exact amount of sugar varies a little on account of size of eggs.

CHOCOLATE CAKE—Cook one cup of sugar, one-half cup of milk, one-half cup of grated chocolate and the beaten yolk of one egg together until smooth. When done add a teaspoon of vanilla and cool. Beat one-half cup of butter to a cream, add one cup of sugar slowly, and beat smooth. Add two beaten eggs, one-half cup of milk, two cups of flour in which two-thirds teaspoon of soda has been sifted and when well beaten add the cool chocolate mixture. Bake in four layers and put together with a white boiled icing.

CHOCOLATE CAKE—Cook one cup of sugar, one-half cup of milk, one cup of grated chocolate and the beaten yolk of one egg together until smooth. When done add a teaspoon of vanilla and cool. Beat one-half cup of butter to a cream, add one cup of sugar slowly and beat smooth. Add two beaten eggs, one-half cup of milk, two cups of flour in which two-thirds teaspoon of soda has been sifted, and when well beaten add the cool chocolate mixture. Bake in four layers and put together with a white boiled icing.

CHOCOLATE LAYER CAKE—Beat a half cupful butter to a cream, adding gradually one cupful sugar. When light beat in a little at a time, a half cupful milk and a teaspoonful vanilla. Beat the whites of six eggs to a stiff froth and sift a teaspoonful and a half with two cupfuls flour. Add the sifted flour to the mixture. Then fold in the whipped whites. Have three buttered layer cake tins ready and put two-thirds of the mixture into two of them, into the third tin put the remainder of the batter, having first added to it two tablespoons melted chocolate Bake the cakes in a rather quick oven for twenty minutes. Put a layer of the white cake on a large plate and cover with white icing, on this lay a dark layer and cover with more of the white icing. On this put the third cake and cover with the chocolate icing. Put into a graniteware pan one cupful and a half cupful water and cook gently until bubbles begin to rise from bottom. Do not stir or shake while cooking. Take at once from the stove and pour in a thin stream over the stiffly whipped whites of two eggs. Beat it until thick, flavor with vanilla, and use two-thirds of this for the white icing. Into the remainder put a tablespoon and a half melted chocolate and a suspicion of cinnamon extract, and frost the top and sides of the cake.

CHOCOLATE LOAF CAKES—Cream one cup of butter, add two and one-half cups of sugar and beat to a cream. Beat the yolks of five eggs light, add to the butter and sugar, with one cup of milk and three cups of flour in which four level teaspoons of baking powder have been sifted, the stiffly beaten whites of five eggs and two teaspoons of vanilla flavoring and two squares of chocolate melted. Bake in a moderate oven.

COCOA CAKE—Cream one-half cup of butter, add one cup of sugar, and beat again. Add the beaten yolks of three eggs and a teaspoon of vanilla. Sift two cups of pastry flour twice with one-quarter cup of cocoa and four level teaspoons of baking powder. Add to the first mixture alternately with three-quarters cup of milk, beat hard, and fold in the stiffly beaten whites of three eggs. Bake in a loaf and cover with white icing.

CREAM CAKE OR PIE—This recipe makes a simple layer cake to be filled in various ways. Cream one-quarter cup of butter with one cup of sugar, add the beaten yolks of two eggs and one teaspoon of vanilla. Now beat hard, then mix in one-half cup of milk alternately with one and one-half cups of flour sifted twice with two level teaspoons of baking powder. Beat just enough to make smooth, then fold in lightly the stiffly beaten whites of two eggs and pour into an oblong shallow pan that is buttered, floured and rapped to shake out all that is superfluous. Bake about twenty minutes, take from pan and cool. Just before serving split the cake and fill with a cooked cream filling or with sweet thick cream beaten, sweetened with powdered sugar and flavored to the taste.

CREAM LAYER CAKE—Cream one-quarter cup of butter well with one cup of sugar, add the yolks of three eggs beaten light, one-half cup of milk, then one and one-half cups of flour sifted twice with three level teaspoons of baking powder. Stir in lightly last of all the whites of three eggs beaten stiff. Bake in a pan large enough to make one thin cake and bake. Cool and split, then spread on one-half pint of cream beaten light, sweetened, and flavored with a few drops of vanilla. Put on the top cake and dust with powdered sugar.

DATE CAKE—Sift two cups of flour with four level teaspoons of baking powder, one-half level teaspoon of salt and one-quarter cup of butter. Beat one egg, add three-quarters cup of milk and mix into the ingredients. Add last one and one-half cups of dates stoned and cut into small pieces and rolled in flour. Bake in a sheet in a moderate oven and serve warm or with a liquid sauce as a pudding.

EGGLESS CAKE—One and one-half cups sugar, one cup sour milk, three cups sifted flour, one-half cup shortening, one teaspoon soda, one-half teaspoon cinnamon, one-half teaspoon nutmeg, one cup chopped raisins, salt.

FEATHER CAKE—Sift one cup of sugar, two cups of sifted flour, three level teaspoons of baking powder and a few grains of salt. Add one cup of milk, one well beaten egg, three table-spoons of melted butter and a teaspoon of vanilla or lemon flavoring or a level teaspoon of mixed spices. Beat hard and bake in a loaf in a moderate oven about half an hour.

FIG CAKE—Two cupfuls of sugar, two-thirds of a cup of butter, one cupful of milk, four even cupfuls of flour, five eggs, two teaspoonfuls of cream of tartar, one of soda, sifted with the flour, mix the butter and sugar until creamed, add the unbeaten yolks of the eggs, add the milk and the flour slowly, beating all the time, lastly the whites of the eggs. Flavor two cupfuls of chopped figs and mix in. Bake quickly.

FIG LAYER CAKE—Cream one-quarter cup of butter with one cup of sugar, add one beaten egg, one cup of milk, two cups of flour sifted twice with four teaspoons of baking powder. Bake in layer tins.

For the filling chop one-half pound of figs fine, add one-half cup of sugar and one-quarter cup of cold water. Cook in a double boiler until soft, let cool, and spread between the cakes.

FRUIT CAKE—One cup dark sugar, one-half cup butter, one cup molasses, one cup coffee (cold liquid), three eggs, three tablespoons mixed spices, one pound currants, two pounds raisins, three cups flour, three teaspoons baking powder, one-fourth pound citron.

GOLD CAKE—Mix the yolks of four eggs, one cup of sugar, one-half cup of sweet milk, one-half cup of butter, three cups of flour sifted three times, one teaspoonful of cream of tartar and half teaspoon of soda. Beat very thoroughly. Use a moderate cake oven.

HICKORY NUT CAKE—Cream one cup of butter with two cups of sugar, add the well beaten yolks of four eggs, and one-half cup of milk. Sift three level teaspoons of baking powder twice with two and one-half cups of pastry flour. Reserve one-half cup of the flour and add the remainder to the first mixture

Now fold in the whites of four eggs beaten stiff, one teaspoon of lemon juice, half a dozen gratings of the yellow rind of lemon and one cup each of seeded and chopped raisins and of chopped hickory nuts mixed with the reserved half cup of flour. Bake in a moderate oven, cover with a white icing and garnish without meats.

HUCKLEBERRY CAKES—Mix together one quart of flour, one teaspoon salt, four teaspoons baking powder and one-half cup of sugar. Mix one-third cup butter, melted with one cup of milk. Add it to the flour and then add enough more milk to make a dough stiff enough to keep in shape when dropped from a spoon. Flour one pint of berries, stir in quickly, and drop by the large spoonful on a buttered pan or in muffin rings. Bake twenty minutes.

ICE CREAM CAKE—Cream three-quarters cup of butter with two cups of fine granulated sugar. Add one cup of milk with two cups of flour and three-quarters cup of cornstarch sifted twice with five level teaspoons of baking powder. Fold in slowly the whites of seven eggs and bake in layers.

LAYER CAKE—One and one-half cups of sugar, two-thirds of a cup of butter, the whites of six eggs, one cup of sweet milk, two and one-half cups of pastry flour, two teaspoonfuls of baking powder, flavor with lemon, put two-thirds of the mixture into jelly tins. To the rest add two tablespoonfuls of molasses, one-half cup of raisins (seeded), three figs (chopped), one teaspoonful cinnamon, one-half teaspoonful allspice, two tablespoonfuls of flour. Bake, when cool, together with jelly, having the dark layer in the center.

MARGARETTES—One-half pound of peanuts, one pound of dates chopped fine. One cup of milk in the dates, and boil, add peanuts. Make a boiled icing. Take the long branch crackers, spread the filling between the crackers, put on the icing, and put in the oven to brown.

PLAIN CAKE—Beat together one-half cup of butter and two cups of sugar until light and creamy, add the well beaten yolks of three eggs, one-half cup of milk, three cups of flour in which three teaspoons of baking powder have been sifted, and last the stiffly beaten whites of three eggs. Add any flavoring preferred and bake in a moderate oven.

PLAIN TEA CAKE—Cream two level tablespoons of butter and one cup of sugar together, add one beaten egg, one cup of milk and two cups of flour in which three level teaspoons of baking powder have been sifted. Bake in a sheet, and serve while fresh.

RAISIN CAKE—One cup butter, three eggs, one and one-half cups sugar, one cup sour milk, one teaspoon soda, one cup raisins, little nutmeg, three cups flour. One can use two eggs and one-half cup butter; then bake as usual.

ROCKLAND CAKE—Two cups sugar, one cup butter beaten to a cream, five eggs, one cup milk, four cups flour, two teaspoonfuls baking powder, one teaspoonful essence of lemon.

SNIPPODOODLES—One cup of sugar, one tablespoon of butter, one-half cup of milk, one egg, one cup of flour, one teaspoon of cinnamon. Cream the butter, add the sugar, shell the eggs well beaten, then the flour, baking powder and cinnamon, sifted together, and the milk. Spread very thin on the tin sheet and bake. When nearly done sprinkle with sugar; when brown remove from the oven, cut into squares and remove quickly with a knife. They should be thin and crispy.

SNOW CAKE—Beat the white of four eggs stiff. Cream one-half cup of milk and one cup of butter and one cup of sugar, add one-half cup of milk and two cups of flour sifted twice with three level teaspoons of baking powder. Fold in the whites of the eggs last and half a teaspoon or more of lemon or vanilla flavoring.

SPICE CAKES—For little spice cakes cream one-half cup of butter with one cup of sugar, add one beaten egg, one-half cup of sour milk, and one-half level teaspoon each of soda, baking powder, and cinnamon, and a few gratings of nutmeg sifted with two and one-half cups of pastry flour. Stir in one-half cup each of chopped walnut meats and seeded and chopped raisins. Roll out thin and cut in shape or put small spoonfuls some distance apart on a buttered pan and press out with the end of a baking powder can until as thin as needed; do not add more flour. Bake slowly.

SPONGE CAKE—Whites of two eggs beaten to a stiff froth, beat the yolks thoroughly, then beat both together, then add one scant cup of granulated sugar (beating again), one scant cup of flour (beat again), and one teaspoon of baking powder. Sift the flour three or four times, stir the baking powder in the flour, and lastly add five tablespoons of hot water.

SULTANA TEA CAKES—Into three-quarters of a pound of flour stir a pinch of salt, a teaspoonful of baking powder, three ounces of butter and lard mixed in equal portions, three ounces of sifted sugar and two ounces of sultanas. Chop one and half ounces of candied lemon peel, add that and moisten all with two well beaten eggs and a little milk if necessary. Work these ingredients together, with a wooden spoon turn on to a board and form into round cakes. Place them on a floured baking sheet and cook in a quick oven. Five minutes before the cakes are done brush them over with milk to form a glaze, and when ready to serve cut each through with a knife and spread liberally with butter

SUNSHINE CAKE—Cream one cup of butter, add two cups of sugar and beat, add one cup of milk, the yolks of eleven eggs beaten until very light and smooth, and three cups of flour sifted with four teaspoons of baking powder three times to make it very light. Turn into a tube baking pan and bake three-quarters of an hour in a moderate oven.

TEA CAKE—This cake is to be eaten warm with butter. Rub a rounding tablespoon of butter into three cups of flour sifted with a saltspoon of salt, six level teaspoons of baking powder and one-quarter cup of sugar. Beat one egg light, add one and one-half cups of milk and the dry ingredients and beat well. Pour into a long buttered pan and bake about twenty minutes. Do not slice this cake, but cut through the crust with a sharp knife and break apart. This mixture can be baked in muffin tins, but it saves time to bake it in a loaf.

VELVET CAKE—One-half cup butter, one and one-half cups sugar, yolks four eggs, one-half cup milk, one and one-half cups flour, one-half cup cornstarch, four level teaspoons baking powder, whites four eggs, one-third cup almonds blanched shredded. Cream the butter, add gradually the sugar, then the egg-yolks well beaten. Beat well and add the milk, the flour, cornstarch, and baking powder sifted together, and egg whites beaten stiff. Beat well and turn into buttered shallow pan. Sprinkle with the almonds, then with powdered sugar and bake forty minutes in a moderate oven.

WHITE PATTY CAKES—Cream one-third cup of butter with one cup of sugar, add one-half cup of milk, one and three-quarter cups of flour sifted twice with two and one-half level teaspoons of baking powder, and flavor with a mixture of one-third teaspoon of lemon flavoring and two-thirds teaspoon of vanilla flavoring. Bake in little plain patty pans and cover the top of each with white icing. Garnish with two little leaves cut from angelica and a bit of red candied cherry.

COFFEE CREAM CAKES AND FILLING—Roll good plain paste three-eighths of an inch thick and cut in rounds and through a pastry tube force a cream cake mixture to make a border come out even with the edge of the round, and bake in a hot oven. Fill and frost. For the cream cake mixture put one cup of boiling water, one-half cup of butter and one level tablespoon of sugar together in a saucepan and boil one minute, then add one and three-quarters cups of flour all at once. Stir rapidly and when the cooked mixture cleaves from the pan add five eggs one at a time, beating well between each addition. Do not beat the eggs before adding.

COFFEE ECLAIRS—Put one cup of hot water, one-half cup of butter and one-half teaspoon of salt in a small saucepan over the fire. The instant it boils add quickly one and one-half cups of sifted pastry flour. Stir thoroughly for five minutes, or till it all clears from the pan in a lump. Let it cool slightly and then add five eggs whole, one at a time. Mix very thoroughly, then drop the dough with a spoon on to a buttered baking pan in pieces about four inches long and one and one-half inches wide and some distance apart. Bake in a quick oven until well puffed up and done through; they will settle as soon as removed if not baked sufficiently. When cool, cut along one edge and fill with the prepared cream and frost with coffee icing.

CRUMPETS—Scald two cups of milk, add four tablespoons of melted butter and when lukewarm one level teaspoon of salt and three and one-half cups of flour. Beat hard, add one-half yeast cake, dissolved in one-half cup of lukewarm water and beat again. Let rise until light, then grease large muffin rings and set them on a hot griddle. Fill each ring not over half full and bake slowly until a light brown, turn rings and contents over, bake a little longer, then slip rings off. Serve hot. If any are left over, split, toast and butter them.

CRULLERS—Scald one cup of milk, and when lukewarm add one yeast cake dissolved in one quarter cup of lukewarm water, and add one and one-half cups of flour and a level teaspoon of salt. Cover and let rise until very light; add one cup of sugar, one-quarter cup of melted butter, three well beaten eggs, one-half of a small nutmeg grated and enough more flour to make a stiff dough. Cover and let rise light, turn on to a floured board and roll out lightly. Cut into long narrow strips and let rise on the board. Now twist the strips and fry until a light brown color, and dust over with powdered sugar.

DUTCH CRULLERS—Cream one cup of sugar and one-half cup of butter, add one egg and beat, then one cup of sour milk. Sift one level teaspoon of flour and add to the mixture, now beat in enough sifted pastry flour to make a dough that can be rolled out. Cut in rings and taking hold of each side of a ring twist it inside out. Fry in deep hot fat.

INDIVIDUAL SHORTCAKES—Sift two cups of flour, three teaspoons of baking powder, and one-half level teaspoon of salt together. Add two well beaten eggs and one-half cup of melted butter. Beat and pour into greased muffin pans until they are two-thirds full. Bake in a hot oven, then split and butter. Crush a quart box of any kind of berries, sprinkle with one-half of cup of sugar and use as a filling for the little short-cakes.

RAISED DOUGHNUTS—Scald one cup of milk. When lukewarm add one-quarter of a yeast cake dissolved in one-quarter of a cup of lukewarm water, one teaspoon salt and flour enough to make a stiff batter. Let it rise over night. In the morning add one-third of a cup of shortening (butter and lard mixed), one cup light brown sugar, two eggs well beaten, one-half nutmeg grated and enough flour to make a stiff dough. Let it rise again, toss on floured board, pat and roll out. Shape with the biscuit cutter and work between the hands until round. Place on the floured board, let rise one hour, turn and let rise again. Fry in deep fat and drain on brown paper. Cool and roll in powdered sugar.

SOUR MILK DOUGHNUTS—Beat two eggs light, add one cup of sugar and beat, one-half cup of butter and lard mixed, and beat again. Stir one level teaspoon of soda into one pint of sour milk, add to the other ingredients and mix with enough sifted pastry flour to make a dough as soft as can be rolled. Take a part at a time, roll half an inch thick, cut in rings and fry. Use nutmeg, cinnamon, or any flavoring liked. These doughnuts are good for the picnic basket or to carry out to the boys at their camp.

SUGAR COOKIES—Beat to a cream one cupful of shortening, half lard and half butter, one cupful granulated sugar. Add one cup rich sour cream and two eggs unbeaten, four cupfuls flour sifted with one teaspoonful soda and a half teaspoonful baking powder. Stir just enough to make a stiff dough, toss on to the lightly floured molding board and knead another cupful of flour into it. This mixing gives the cookies a fine grain. Flavor with a little nutmeg, roll out, cut into cookies, and bake.

SOFT GINGER COOKIES—Put a level teaspoon of soda in a measuring cup, add three tablespoons of boiling water, one-quarter cup of melted butter or lard, a saltspoon of salt, a level teaspoon of ginger, and enough sifted pastry flour to make a dough as soft as can be handled. Shape small bits of dough, lay in the greased baking pan and press out half an inch thick; bake carefully.

For Your
Children's Sake
Look
For

ZATEK
Milk Chocolate
EATMORS

Now more than ever are these pure chocolate morsels appreciated by big brothers, big sisters and parents. With epidemics rapidly spreading all over the country, one naturally hesitates to give children candy scooped out of a pail or pan and frequently handled.

Not so with ZATEK Milk Chocolate EATMORS. There are 28 or more sweet milk chocolate tid-bits in each dust-tight tube. Packed by machinery at the factory and untouched by hand. They always reach you crisp and fresh, pure, sweet and wholesome. EATMORS are easy to divide equally among children. You can give your children ZATEK Milk Chocolate EATMORS with perfect safety.

Sold by druggists and confectioners.

PENNSYLVANIA CHOCOLATE CO.
Pittsburgh, U. S. A.

FOR YOUR CHILDREN'S SAKE, READERS ARE
URGED TO CHOOSE ZATEK MILK CHOCOLATE EATMORS
IN THIS 1916 ADVERTISEMENT.

"Ameyea or itinerant candy vender," by Robert Frederick Blum (1857–1903) around 1894, the year Mr. Rufus Estes was in Japan for the Cherry Blossom Festival.

Photograph courtesy of the Library of Congress.

CANDIES

CANDIED VIOLETS—Gather the required quantity of perfect sweet violets, white or blue. If possible, pick in the early morning while the dew is still on them. Spread on an inverted sieve and stand in the air until dried, but not crisp. Make a sirup, using a half pound of pure granulated sugar and a half pint of water. Cook without stirring until it spins a thread. Take each violet by the stem, dip into the hot sirup and return to the sieve, which should be slightly oiled. Leave for several hours. If the flowers then look preserved and clear they will not require a second dipping, but if they appear dry as if some portions of the petals were not properly saturated, dip again. Now have ready a half cupful of melted fondant. Add a drop or two of violet extract and a few drops of water to reduce the fondant to a thin, grayish, paste-like consistency. Dip the flowers in this one at a time, dust with powdered crystallized sugar, and lay on oiled paper to harden. Rose leaves may be candied in the same way, substituting essence of rose for the violet and a drop or two of cochineal to make the required color. A candy dipper or fine wire can he used for dipping the rose petals.

CREAMED WALNUTS—Cook two cups of sugar and one-half cup of water together until the sirup threads. Add a teaspoon of vanilla, take from the range and beat until thick and creamy. Make small balls of the candy and press half a walnut meat into each side. Drop on to a plate of granulated sugar.

CRYSTALLIZED COWSLIPS—These make a prized English confection, much used for ornamenting fancy desserts. The flowers are gathered when in full bloom, washed gently and placed on a screen to dry. When this is accomplished the stems are cut to within two inches of the head and the flowers are then laid heads down on the tray of the crystallizing tin, pushing the stalks through so the flowers shall be upright. When full put the tray in the deep tin and fill with the same crystallizing sirup, pouring around the sides and not over the flowers. When dry, arrange in baskets or use in decorating.

FRUIT PASTE—Take equal weights of nut meats, figs, dates and prepared seedless raisins. Wipe the figs and remove the stems, remove the scales and stones from the dates. Mix well and chop fine or run it all through a meat chopper. Mold it on a board in confectioners' sugar until you have a smooth, firm paste. Roll out thin and cut into inch squares or small rounds. Roll the edge in sugar, then pack them away in layers with paper between the layers.

GLACE FIGS—Make a sirup by boiling together two cups of sugar and one and a half cups of water. Wash and add as many figs as can be covered by the sirup. Cook until they are tender and yellow, then remove from the fire and let them stand in the sirup over night. In the morning cook for thirty minutes, and again let them stand over night. Then cook until the stems are transparent. When cold drain and lay them on a buttered cake rack or wire broiler and let them remain until very dry.

PINEAPPLE MARSHMALLOWS—This is a good confection for Thanksgiving. Soak four ounces gum arabic in one cupful pineapple juice until dissolved. Put into a granite sauce-pan with a half pound of powdered sugar, and set in a larger pan of hot water over the fire. Stir until the mixture is white and thickened. Test by dropping a little in cold water. If it "balls," take from the fire and whip in the stiffly whipped whites of three eggs. Flavor with a teaspoonful vanilla or orange juice, then turn into a square pan that has been dusted with cornstarch. The mixture should be about an inch in thick-ness. Stand in a cold place for twelve hours, then cut into inch squares and roll in a mixture of cornstarch and powdered sugar.

RAISIN FUDGE—Put into a saucepan one heaped table-spoon butter, melt and add one-half cup milk, two cups sugar, one-fourth cup molasses and two squares chocolate grated. Boil until it is waxy when dropped into cold water. Remove from fire, beat until creamy, then add one-half cup each of chopped raisins and pecans. Pour into a buttered tin, and when cool mark into squares.

SIMPLE WAY OF SUGARING FLOWERS—A simple way of sugaring flowers where they are to be used at once consists in making the customary sirup and cooking to the crack

Eating ice cream sandwiches on the beach in Atlantic City, New Jersey, circa 1890 to 1900.

Photograph courtesy of the Library of Congress.

During most of the 1800s, ice was cut from lakes, hauled ashore using teams of horses, and kept in cold storage until needed. The exceptionally mild winter of 1889 encouraged the rise of ice making plants like the one pictured above. Home refrigerators weren't available until 1916, but most people couldn't afford the price ... $900, roughly what they'd pay for an automobile.

Photographer and date unknown.

degree. Rub the inside of cups with salad oil, put into each cup four tablespoonfuls of the flowers and sugar, let stand until cold, turn out, and serve piled one on top of the other.

ICE CREAM AND SHERBETS

BALTIMORE ICE CREAM—Two quarts of strawberries, two cups of granulated sugar, half cup powdered sugar, one pint cream, about two spoonfuls vanilla, half cup chopped nuts, heat the berries and sugar together, when cool mix other ingredients and freeze.

BLACK CURRANT ICE CREAM—Stew one cupful black currants five minutes, then press through a fine sieve. Add a cupful rich sirup and a cupful thick cream, beat well, then freeze. When stiff pack in an ornamental mold, close over and pack in ice and salt. When ready to serve turn out on a low glass dish, garnish with crystallized cherries and leaves of angelica.

FROZEN ICE—Cook one cup of rice in boiling salted water twelve minutes. Drain and put it in the double boiler, one quart milk, one cup sugar and one saltspoon salt. Cook till soft, then rub through a sieve. Scald one pint of cream and mix with it the beaten yolks of four eggs. Cook about two minutes, or until the eggs are scalding hot, then stir this into the rice. Add more sugar, if needed, and one tablespoonful vanilla. Chill and pack firmly in the freezer or round the mold. Turn out and ornament the top with fresh pineapple cut in crescent pieces or with quartered peaches and serve a fresh fruit sirup sauce with the cream.

FRUIT ICE—Three lemons, three oranges, three bananas, three cups sugar, three pints cold water, by pressing juice from orange and lemons, strain well, peel banana, rub through strainer into the fruit juice, add the sugar, then the water, stir until the sugar is dissolved, pour into freezer. The ice that is used should be pounded until fine, and the right kind of salt should be used.

ICE CREAM WITH MAPLE SAUCE—Scald one quart of cream, add one-half cup of sugar, a bit of salt, and when cold freeze as usual, first flavoring with vanilla or extract of ginger. Reduce some pure maple sirup by boiling until quite thick, stir into it some sliced pecans or walnuts and serve hot with each portion of the cream.

PINEAPPLE CREAM—Two cups of water, one cup of sugar, boil fifteen minutes, let cool, add one can grated pineapple. Freeze to mush, fold in one-half pint of whipped cream, let stand an hour, but longer time is better.

VANILLA ICE CREAM—Put two cups of milk in a double boiler, add a pinch of soda and scald, beat four eggs light with two cups of sugar, pour the hot milk on slowly, stirring all the time; turn back into double boiler and cook until a smooth custard is formed. Cool and flavor strongly with vanilla because freezing destroys some of the strength of flavoring. Stir in a pint of sweet cream and freeze.

CRANBERRY SHERBET—This is often used at a Thanksgiving course dinner to serve after the roast. To make it boil a quart of cranberries with two cupfuls of water until soft, add two cupfuls sugar, stir until dissolved, let cool, add the juice of one or two lemons and freeze. This may be sweeter if desired. Serve in sherbet glasses.

CURRANT SHERBET—Mash ripe red currants well and strain the juice. To two cups of the juice add two cups of sugar, two cups of water, and bring to boiling point. Cook a few minutes and skim well, then pour while hot slowly on to the whites of two eggs beaten stiff. Beat a few minutes, cool, and freeze.

LEMON GINGER SHERBET—This is made the same as the lemon with the addition of four ounces of candied ginger cut in fine bits and added to the sirup with the grated yellow rind of a lemon. Boil until clear, add lemon juice and a little more of the rind and proceed as with the ice.

LEMON SHERBET—Put two cups of sugar into four cups of water and cook five minutes after it begins to boil. Add one-half level tablespoon of gelatin soaked in a tablespoon of cold water for fifteen minutes. Stir one cup of lemon juice and freeze.

PINEAPPLE SORBET—Peel and cut up a small sugar loaf pineapple and let it stand in a cool place over night with a pint of sugar added to it. An earthen jar is best for holding the pine, whose acid properties forbid its standing in tin. In the morning strain, pressing out as much of the juice as possible. Add to this a pint of water and the grated rind of an orange. Boil ten minutes, add the juice of one lemon and two oranges, freeze about fifteen minutes until of a smooth, even, cream-like texture, and serve after the meat course at dinner. If you desire a granite which is frozen as hard as ice cream, but should be of a rough-grained consistency, set the mixture away packed in ice and let it remain there for two or three hours. Scrape the frozen part occasionally from the sides of the can and stir long enough to mix the ice with the mass, but not long enough to make it creamy. Serve in a cup made of the half skin of an orange with the pulp scraped out.

TEA SHERBET—Make a quart of fine flavored tea in the usual way, pour off, sweeten to taste, add the juice of half a lemon and the fine shredded peel, and freeze.

GLACE DES GOURMETS—Make a custard of one pint milk, six egg yolks, one cup sugar and a few grains of salt. Strain and add one pint cream, one cup almonds (blanched, cooked in caramel, cooled, and pounded), and one tablespoon vanilla. Whip one pint heavy cream and add one-half pound powdered sugar, one tablespoon of rum, one teaspoon of vanilla and one-fourth pound of macaroons broken in small pieces. Freeze the first mixture and put in a brick mold, cover with second mixture, then repeat. Pack in salt and ice, using two parts crushed ice to one part rock salt and let stand two hours. Remove from mold and garnish with macaroons in brandy.

MAPLE PARFAIT—Beat four eggs slightly in a double boiler, pour in one cup of hot maple sirup, stirring all the time. Cook until thick, cool, and add one pint of thick cream beaten stiff. Pour into a mold and peek in equal parts of ice and salt. Let stand three hours.

PINEAPPLE PARFAIT—Cook for five minutes over the fire one cup granulated sugar and a quarter cup of water. Beat the yolks of six eggs until lemon colored and thick, then add the sirup little by little, constantly beating. Cook in a double boiler until the custard coats the spoon, then strain and beat until cold. Add two cupfuls pineapple pulp pressed through a sieve and fold in a pint of cream whipped stiff. Pack and bury in the ice and salt mixture.

STRAWBERRY PARFAIT—Hull, wash and drain some sweet strawberries. Press through a strainer enough to give about two-thirds of a cup of pulp. Cook together in a granite-ware saucepan one cupful granulated sugar and half a cup of water until it spins a thread. Do not stir while cooking. Whip two whites of eggs stiff and then pour the hot sirup over them and continue beating them until the mixture is cold. As it thickens add the crushed berries, a spoonful at a time. Have ready a pint of cream whipped to a solid froth, stir lightly into the egg and berry mixture, then pack into a covered mold and bury in ice and salt, equal proportions, leaving it for several hours.

VIOLET PARFAIT—This is made the same as white parfait, using one-third cup of grape juice instead of the boiling water, and adding half a cup of grape juice and the juice of half a lemon to the cream before beating.

VANILLA PARFAIT—Cook a half cup each sugar and water over the fire until it threads. Do not stir after the sugar has dissolved. Beat the whites of three eggs until very stiff, pour the sirup slowly over it, beating constantly. Flavor with vanilla, and when cold fold in a pint of cream whipped stiff. Pour into a mold and pack.

ENTERPRISE

Sausage Stuffer, Lard and Fruit Press

No. 25, 4 qt., $5.50

8 Sizes and Styles. Tinned or Japanned.

$3.75 to $8.50.

POINTS OF MERIT

The Iron Cylinder is bored True, so that **the Plunger plate** fits perfectly in the cylinder, from top to bottom.

Lips on Tin Cylinder, make burning of hands an impossibility.

Corrugations in spout prevent air entering **Casing, thus** assuring preservation of sausage. The only Stuffer possessing this feature, which is Patented.

It can also be used as a fruit press for making **wines, jellies,** etc., from berries of all kinds, Grapes, Currants, Quinces, Pineapples, etc.

The Enterprise Sausage Stuffer, Lard and Fruit Press was available in 8 sizes and styles in 1906.

A WIDER VARIETY OF FRUITS AND VEGETABLES WERE USED IN
PRESERVES, PICKLES AND RELISHES DURING THE LATE
19TH CENTURY AND EARLY 20TH CENTURY.

Illustrator unknown

PRESERVES, PICKLES AND RELISH

CHERRY PICKLES—Stem, but do not pit, large ripe cherries. Put into a jar and cover with a sirup made from two cups of sugar, two cups of vinegar and a rounding teaspoon each of ground cloves and cinnamon cooked together five minutes. Let stand two days, pour off the vinegar, reheat and pour over the cherries, then seal.

CHILI SAUCE—Peel and slice six large ripe tomatoes, add four onions chopped fine, three-quarters of a cup of brown sugar, one-quarter cup of salt, four cups of vinegar and two teaspoons each of ginger and cloves and one-half teaspoon of cayenne pepper. Cook together one hour and seal in small glass jars.

COLD CATSUP—Cut four quarts of tomatoes fine, add one cup of chopped onion, one cup of nasturtium seeds that have been cut fine, one cup of freshly grated horseradish, three large stalks of celery chopped, one cup of whole mustard seeds, one-half cup of salt, one tablespoonful each of black pepper, cloves and cinnamon, a tablespoon of mace, one-half cup of sugar and four quarts of vinegar. Mix all well together and put in jars or bottles. It needs no cooking, but must stand several weeks to ripen.

CREOLE SAUCE—Scald and peel twenty-four tomatoes. Remove the seeds from green peppers and cut the pulp and four onions fine. Shred one ounce dried ginger, mix and add four tablespoons each of sugar and salt, three cups of vinegar and one-half pound seedless raisins. Boil slowly three hours, then put away in wide-mouthed bottles.

GINGERED GREEN TOMATOES—To one peck small green tomatoes allow eight onions. Slice all together and sprinkle with one cupful of salt. Let them stand twenty-four hours, then drain and cover with fresh water. Make a strong ginger tea, allowing one quart of boiling water to a pound of bruised ginger root. Let it simmer gently for twenty minutes until the strength of the ginger is extracted. Scald the chopped tomatoes in this. Drain. Mix together one ounce ground ginger, two tablespoonfuls black pepper, two teaspoonfuls ground cloves, a quarter pound white mustard seed, one-half cupful ground mustard, one ounce allspice, three ounces celery seed and three pounds brown sugar. Now put the sliced onions and tomatoes in a kettle with sugar and spices in alternate layers, and pour over them enough white wine vinegar to cover well. Cook the pickle until tender, then pack in jars and seal.

GREEN TOMATO MINCE—To two quarts chopped apples, greenings are best, allow two quarts chopped green tomatoes, one pound each seeded raisins and cleaned currants, one-half nutmeg, one teaspoonful of cinnamon, one-half teaspoonful ground cloves, six cups granulated sugar and a cupful and a half of cider vinegar. Boil slowly three or four hours and can.

PICALILLI—Allow to one gallon sliced green tomatoes one pint grated horseradish, eleven ounces brown sugar, two tablespoons each of fine salt and ground mustard. Put the tomatoes in a large stone crock, sprinkle the salt over them and let stand over night with a slight press on top. In the morning add to the tomatoes and let stand several weeks until it has formed its own vinegar. Always keep the pickle under the liquor and have it in a cool place.

PEPPER RELISH—Chop fine a small head of white cabbage, six large green peppers, and a nice bunch of celery. Put in a large bowl and sprinkle with a half cup of salt, mix well, cover and let stand over night. Next morning drain and mix in two tablespoons of mustard seed, and pack in a stone jar. Put in a porcelain kettle three pints of vinegar, two tablespoons sugar, one tablespoon each of whole cloves, allspice and whole pepper, a clove of garlic and one onion minced. Simmer gently twenty minutes, strain and pour boiling hot over the vegetables. When cold cover and keep in a cool place.

TOMATO CATSUP—This catsup has a good relish on account of the onion in it. Wash ripe tomatoes, cut them in slices and cook slowly for one hour. Press through a sieve to take out the seeds and skin. To one quart of this pulp and juice add one tablespoon of cinnamon, one of black pepper and one of mustard, one teaspoon of cayenne, one-half cup of salt and two onions chopped fine. Simmer two and one-half hours, then add two cups of vinegar, cook an hour longer. Put in bottles and seal.

TOMATO CHUTNEY—Cut up and peel twelve large to-matoes and to them add six onions chopped fine, one cup of vinegar, one cup of sugar, a handful of finely chopped raisins, salt to taste, a half teaspoonful of cayenne and a half teaspoonful of white pepper. boil one and one-half hours and bottle or put in stone jars.

VEGETABLE RELISH—Use two quarts each of cooked and finely chopped beets and cabbage, add four cups sugar, two tablespoons salt, one tablespoon black pepper, a half tablespoon of cayenne, a cup of grated horseradish and enough cold vinegar to cover. Bottle in glass jars and keep in a cool place.

APPLE AND GRAPE JELLY—Pull the grapes off the stems of six large bunches, put them in a preserving kettle, just cover with water. Pare and slice six large fall pippin apples. Put them with the grapes. When boiled soft strain through a flannel bag. To a pint of juice allow three quarters of a pound of sugar. Boil the juice fifteen minutes, skim and add the sugar, which has been heated. Boil ten or fifteen minutes. This will fill three jelly glasses.

BLACK CURRANT JELLY—This is one of the best old-fashioned remedies for sore throats, while a teaspoonful of it dissolved into a tumbler of cold water affords a refreshing fever drink or family beverage on a hot day. Stem large ripe black currants and after washing put into the preserving kettle, allow-ing a cupful of water to each quart of fruit. This is necessary because the black currant is drier than the red or white. Mash with a wooden spoon or pestle, then cover and cook until the currants have reached the boiling point and are soft. Turn into a jelly bag and drain without squeezing. To each pint of the juice allow a half pound loaf sugar. Stir until well mixed, then cook just ten minutes from the time it commences to boil. Overcooking makes it tough and stringy. Pour in sterilized glasses and when cold cover with paraffin.

CANNED PINEAPPLE—Pare the pineapple and carefully remove the eyes with a sharp-pointed silver knife. Chop or grate or shred it with a fork, rejecting the core. Weigh, and to every pound of fruit allow a half pound of sugar, put all together in the preserving kettle, bring quickly to boiling, skim, and remove at once. Put into jars and fill to overflowing with sirup, and seal.

CHERRY PRESERVES—Select large red cherries, stem and stone them, and save the juice. Weigh the fruit and an equal amount of sugar. Sprinkle the sugar over the cherries and let stand six hours, then put into a preserving kettle, add the juice, and heat slowly. Simmer until the cherries are clear, and skim carefully several times. Seal in jars and keep in a cool, dark place.

CRANBERRY CONSERVE—To three and a half pounds cranberries add three pounds sugar, one pound seeded raisins and four oranges, cut in small pieces after peeling. Cook gently about twenty minutes, take from the fire, add one pound walnut meats, and cool.

CHERRY JELLY—The juice of cherries does not make a firm jelly without the addition of gelatin. This means that it will not keep, but must be eaten soon after making. But if a soft jelly will satisfy it can be made, and kept like other jellies, without gelatin. To make this jelly crush ripe cherries and cook until soft, with just enough water to keep from burning. Strain and measure, to each cup of juice allow a cup of sugar. Simmer the juice ten minutes, heat the sugar and drop into the boiling juice. In a few minutes a soft jelly will form.

CRANBERRY MOLD—This is an extremely pretty way of serving cranberries in individual molds. Wash a quart of cran-berries and put in a porcelain or granite saucepan. Sprinkle over the top of the berries two cupfuls of sugar and on top of the sugar pour one cupful cold water. Set over the fire and cook slowly. When the berries break into a boil, cover just a few moments, not long, or the skins will burst, then uncover and cook until tender. Do not strain, but pour at once into small china molds. This gives a dark rich looking mold that is not too acid and pre-serves the individuality of the fruit. If you wish to use some of the cranberries in lieu of Maraschino cherries, take up some of the most perfect berries before they have cooked too tender, us-ing a darning needle or clean hat pin to impale them. Spread on an oiled plate and set in warning oven or a sunny window until candied.

CURRANT AND RASPBERRY JELLY—Some of the fin-est jellies and jams are made from raspberries combined with currants. For jelly use two-thirds of currant juice to one-third raspberry juice and finish in the usual way.

FIG PRESERVES—Take the figs when nearly ripe and cut across the top in the form of a cross. Cover with strong salted water and let stand three days, changing the water every day. At the end of this time cover with fresh water, adding a few grape or fig leaves to color, and cook until quite green. Then put again in cold water, changing twice daily, and leave three days longer. Add a pound granulated sugar to each pound figs, cook a few moments, take from the fire and set aside for two days. Add more sugar to make sweet, with sliced and boiled lemon or ginger root to flavor, and cook until tender and thick.

GREEN GRAPE MARMALADE—If, as often happens, there are many unripened grapes still on the vines and frost threatens, gather them all and try this green grape marmalade. Take one gallon stemmed green grapes, wash, drain and put on to cook in a porcelain kettle with one pint of water. Cook until soft, rub through a sieve, measure and add an equal amount of sugar to the pulp. Boil hard twenty-five minutes, watching closely that it does not burn, then pour into jars or glasses. When cold cover with melted paraffin, the same as for jelly.

GREEN TOMATOES CANNED FOR PIES—To fifteen pounds round green tomatoes sliced thin allow nine pounds granulated sugar and a quarter pound ginger, washed, scraped and cut very thin, and four lemons scrubbed and sliced thin, removing all seeds. Put this mixture over the fire with a pint of water and cook about half an hour, taking care the contents of the kettle do not scorch. Turn into sterilized glass jars and seal air tight. A tablespoonful of cinnamon and a half tablespoonful each of cloves and allspice may be added to the sauce while cooking if desired.

PEAR AND BLUEBERRY PRESERVES—Pick over and wash two quarts of blueberries, add water to nearly cover and stew them half hour. Mash them well, when all are broken turn into a bowl covered with cheese cloth. Drain well and when cool squeeze out all the juice. Put the blueberry juice on to boil, add one pint of sugar to each pint of juice and remove all scum. Allow one quart of sliced pears to one pint of juice. Use hard pears not suitable for canning. Cook them in the syrup, turning over often and when soft and transparent skim them out into the jars. Boil down the syrup and strain over the fruit. Fill to overflowing and seal.

PRESERVED CURRANTS—Weigh seven pounds of currants before picking over, then stem them and throw out all that are not perfect. Put seven pounds of sugar with three pints of currant juice and boil three minutes, add the currants, one pound of seeded raisins, and cook all twenty minutes. Seal in small jars.

PRESERVED STRAWBERRIES—The following method for preserving strawberries is highly recommended. Weigh the berries and allow an equal amount of sugar. As two cups weigh a pound, the sugar can be measured. Put the sugar into the preserving kettle with enough cold water to moisten it, but not enough to make it a liquid. Set the kettle on the back of the range, and when the sugar has entirely dissolved lay in the fruit and heat. As soon as it boils skim and cook five minutes. Do not stir or mash the berries. Now spread them around on deep platters or enameled pans and cover with panes of window glass. Set in the sun, and the syrup will gradually thicken. Turn into small jars and seal.

RHUBARB JAM—Add to each pound of rhubarb cut without peeling, a pound of sugar and one lemon. Pare the yellow peel from the lemon, taking care to get none of the bitter white pith. Slice the pulp of the lemon in an earthen bowl, discarding the seeds. Put the rhubarb into the bowl with the sugar and lemon, cover and stand away in a cool place over night. In the morning turn into the preserving kettle, simmer gently three-quarters of an hour or until thick, take from the fire, cool a little and pour into jars.

SPICED CRABAPPLES—Wash the crabapples, cut out the blossoms end with a silver knife. To four pounds of fruit take two pounds of sugar, one pint of vinegar, one heaping teaspoon each of broken cinnamon, cassia buds and allspice, add one scant tablespoon whole cloves. Tie the spices in a thin bag and boil with the vinegar and sugar five minutes. Skim them add the apples and simmer slowly until tender; which will take about ten or fifteen minutes. Skim out the apples, putting them in a large bowl or jar. Boil the sugar five minutes longer and pour over the fruit. Next day drain off the syrup, heat to the boiling point and pour again over the apples. Do this for the next two days, then bottle and seal while hot.

SPICED CRABAPPLE JELLY—With crabapples still on hand a nice spiced jelly can be made to serve with meats. Cook the apples without peeling until tender. Strain through a jelly bag, add vinegar to taste with cloves and cinnamon. Cook twen-ty minutes, add an equal quantity of sugar that has been heated in the oven. Boil five minutes, skim and turn in glasses.

SPICED RIPE TOMATO—Peel ripe tomatoes and weigh. For each seven pounds allow two cups of vinegar, seven cups of sugar, one ounce of whole allspice, the same of stick cinnamon and one-half ounces of whole cloves. Cook the tomatoes half an hour or until soft, cutting to pieces while cooking. Add the vinegar, sugar and spices tied in a muslin bag. Cook until thick like marmalade. Serve with cold meats.

TOMATO FIGS—Scald eight pounds of yellow tomatoes and remove the skins. Pack them in layers with an equal weight of sugar. After twenty-four hours drain off the juice and simmer five minutes, add the tomatoes and boil until clear. Remove the fruit with a skimmer and harden in the sun while you boil down the syrup until thick; pack jars two-thirds full of the tomatoes, pour the syrup over and seal. Add the juice of four lemons, two ounces of green ginger root tied up in a bag and the parboiled yellow rind of the lemons to the juice when boiling down.

WILD GRAPE BUTTER—If the wild frost grapes are used, take them after the frost has ripened them. Stem and mash, then mix with an equal quantity of stewed and mashed apple. Rub the mixture through a sieve, add half as much sugar as there is pulp and cook until thick, being careful that it does not burn. It is a good idea to set preserves and fruit butters in the oven with the door ajar to finish cooking as there is then much less danger of burning or spattering.

YELLOW TOMATO PRESERVES—Allow a pound sugar to each pound tomatoes and half cup of water to each pound fruit. Cover the tomatoes with boiling water, then skim. Make a syrup with the sugar, and when boiling skim and add the tomatoes. Have ready a sliced lemon that has been cooked in boiling water and a little sliced ginger. Add to the tomatoes. Cook until the tomatoes are clear, remove, pack in jars, cook the syrup until thick, pour over and seal.

MINCE MEAT—One peck sour apples, three pounds boiled beef, two pounds suet, one quart canned cherries, one quart grape juice, one pint cider, one pint apple butter, one glass orange marmalade, half pound candied orange peel, half pound citron, two pounds currants, two pounds raisins, two tablespoonfuls salt. Put all together and boil up well. This may be canned for future use.

SOUFFLES

ASPARAGUS SOUFFLE—Only very tender asparagus should be used. Cut it fine and boil tender in salted water. Add the well beaten yolks of four eggs, one tablespoonful of soft butter, a saltspoon of salt and a little pepper. Then fold in the stiffly beaten whites of the eggs and bake in a steady oven. Canned asparagus can be substituted for fresh.

CABBAGE SOUFFLE—Chop a solid white head of cabbage and cook in salted water until tender. Drain and place in a buttered dish in layers with a sprinkling of grated cheese between. Mix two tablespoonfuls each of flour and butter, add one cupful of rich milk, the beaten yolks of two eggs and a saltspoon of salt and mustard, stir over the fire until it boils. Then add the stiffly beaten whites of the eggs, pour over the cabbage and bake for half an hour.

CHEESE SOUFFLE—Mix together one-half cup breadcrumbs, a quarter teaspoon salt, a half teaspoonful mustard and a dash of cayenne. Add a tablespoonful butter, a cup and a half milk and cook over hot water. When heated remove. Add while hot two cups grated cheese and the well beaten yolks of three eggs. Cool. When ready to bake add the beaten whites of four eggs and a cup of whipped cream. Fill individual cups half full, set in a pan of hot water and bake fifteen minutes in a quick oven.

CORN SOUFFLE—To one pint of sweet grated corn (canned corn) drain and run through a food chopper (may be used), add the well beaten yolks of two eggs, one pint of sweet milk, one small teaspoonful of salt, one and one-half tablespoonfuls of sugar and the stiffly beaten whites of the eggs. Mix well and bake in a buttered casserole or ramequins for forty minutes.

GUERNSEY CHEESE SOUFFLE—Pin a narrow folded paper thoroughly buttered on the inside, around six or eight ramequins and butter the ramequins thoroughly. Melt two tablespoonfuls butter and in it cook two tablespoonfuls of flour and a quarter teaspoonful each of salt and paprika. When the

WATKINS' POULTRY TONIC

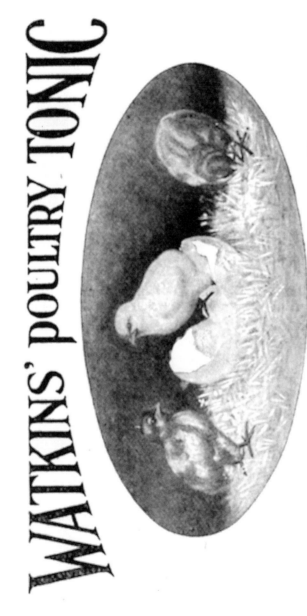

HELPS TO MAKE CHICKS GROW

Watkins' Poultry Tonic Helps To Make Chicks Grow, according to this advertisement in *Watkins' Home Doctor & Cook Book* of 1913.

EASTER CARDS POSTMARKED 1908 AND 1909 RESPECTIVELY.

mixture looks frothy stir in half a cup of milk and stir until boiling. Then add four ounces grated cheese and the beaten yolks of three eggs. Lastly fold in the stiffly whipped whites of three eggs. Put the mixture into the ramequins letting it come up to the paper or nearly to the top of the dishes. Set the ramequins on many folds of paper in a dish, pour in boiling water to half fill, and let bake in a moderate oven until the mixture is well puffed up and firm to the touch. Remove the buttered paper, set the ramequins in place and serve at once. A green vegetable salad seasoned with French dressing and a browned cracker may accompany the dish.

SOUFFLE OF CARROTS—Boil the carrots and mash them fine, add a little sugar to taste, a pinch of salt, a spoonful of flour and a good lump of butter, the well beaten yolks of four eggs, and lastly fold in the stiffly beaten whites. Bake in a quick oven in the dish in which it may be served.

TOMATO SOUFFLE—Stew three cupfuls of tomato down to two, add seasoning to taste and six eggs, the whites beaten stiff, and bake for ten or fifteen minutes or until set. Serve as soon as done.

FILLING FOR CAKES

COFFEE CREAM FOR CHARLOTTE AND ECLAIR—Flavor one pint of rich thick cream with one-fourth cup of black coffee and one teaspoon of lemon, add about a half a cup of sugar, chill and whip it until thick enough to stand. Pour it into molds lined with thin sponge cake or lady fingers. Fill them level and ornament the top with some of the cream forced through tube.

FILLING—For the filling scald one cup of milk with three level tablespoons of ground coffee and let stand where it will be hot but not boil, for five minutes. Strain, add one-half cup of sugar, three level tablespoons of flour and a pinch of salt. Cook in a double boiler fifteen minutes, add one beaten egg and cook two minutes, stirring to keep smooth. Cool and add one-quarter teaspoon of vanilla flavoring. Fill the cream cakes and cover with cream beaten thick, sweetened with powdered sugar and flavored with a few drops of vanilla.

FILLING FOR CAKE—Soak a level tablespoon of gelatin in one tablespoon of cold water for half an hour, add one tablespoon of boiling water and stir. Heat one pint of cream stiff, then beat in the soaked gelatin, add powdered sugar to make sweet and a small teaspoon vanilla flavoring or enough to suit the taste. Put this filling in thick layers between the cakes and cover the top one with a white icing.

FIG OR DATE FROSTING—These frostings are excellent to use upon any kind of cake, but as they are rather rich in themselves, they seem better suited for light white cake. If figs are preferred they should be chopped fine. If dates, the stones and as much as possible of the white lining should be removed and then they should be chopped fine. For a good size loaf of cake, baked in two layers, use a scant quarter of a pound of either the chopped dates or figs, put into a double boiler or saucepan with a very little boiling water, just enough to make the mass pliable. Let them stand and heat while the syrup is boiling. For this two cups of fine granulated sugar and half a cup of boiling water are required. Boil without stirring till the syrup taken upon the spoon or skewer will "thread." Do not allow it to boil too hard at first. When the sugar is thoroughly melted, move the saucepan to a hotter part of the stove so that it may boil more vigorously. Have ready the whites of two eggs beaten dry, now to them add the fig or date paste and pour the boiling syrup in a fine stream over the two, beating all the time. Beat occasionally while cooling, and when thoroughly cold add one teaspoonful of lemon extract, and it is ready for use. These frostings may be a trifle sticky the day they are made, especially if the syrup is not boiled very long, but the stickiness disappears by the second day, even if kept in a stone jar.

LEMON JELLY—Grate two lemons, add the juice, one cup of white sugar, one large spoonful of butter and the yolks of three eggs. Stir constantly over the fire until it jellies, when cold spread between cakes.

MAPLE ICING—Scrape half a pound of maple sugar and melt, add two tablespoons of boiling water. While hot pour over the cake. Be sure to melt the sugar before adding the water.

MOCHA FILLING AND ICING—A rich but much liked filling for small cakes is made by boiling one cup of sugar and one-half cup of very strong or very black coffee together until the syrup will thread. In the meantime wash one cup of sweet but-

This is the Jell-O package

THE DELICIOUS DESSERT

JELL-O

NET WGT.   TRADE MARK REG. U.S. PAT. OFF.   3¼ OZS.

A MIXTURE

DELICATE   **DELIGHTFUL**   **DAINTY**

PRICE   **LEMON**   10¢

PURE FRUIT FLAVOR

THE GENESEE PURE FOOD CO.
LE ROY, N.Y.

GOLD MEDALS. ST. LOUIS '04. PORTLAND '05. JAMESTOWN '07. SEATTLE '09

Anything Sold in Any Other Package is Not Jell-O

And the famous Jell-O desserts cannot be made of anything that is not sold and delivered in this package.

There are other 10-cent dessert preparations, but the careful housewife will not take them when the same money buys Jell-O itself.

If any "directions" besides those on the back of the Jell-O package are needed, they will be found in the little booklet in every package.

NIAGARA LITHO. CO. BUFFALO

JELL-O'S ADVERTISING COOKBOOK FROM AROUND 1914 TOUTS THE MERITS OF JELL-O DESERT, JELL-O ICE CREAM POWDER AND CLAIMS "THE JELL-O PRICE NEVER GOES UP, BUT IS ALWAYS 10 CENTS A PACKAGE."

MANY COOKBOOKS FROM THE 1800S AND 1900S CONTAIN RECIPES
FOR ACHES, PAINS, AND COLICKY BABIES. THIS AD FROM
1899 CLAIMS DR. AYER'S CHERRY PECTORAL PLASTER WILL
PREVENT PNEUMONIA AND CURE A LAME BACK.

ter in cold water to take out all the salt. Put in a piece of cheese-cloth and pat it until all the moisture is dried out. Beat until creamy, adding slowly the beaten yolk of one egg and the syrup. Spread this filling between layer cakes, but it is more often used to pipe over the top of small cakes.

ORANGE FILLING—One-half cup of sugar, two and one-half level tablespoons flour, grated rind of one-half orange, one-third cup of orange juice, one tablespoon lemon juice, one egg beaten slightly, one teaspoon melted butter. Mix the ingredients and cook in double boiler for twelve minutes, stirring constantly. Cool before using.

DESERTS

APPLES STUFFED WITH DATES—Core large, slightly acid apples and fill with stoned dates. Pour over them equal parts of sugar and water boiled together. Baste the apples frequently while baking. Serve as a dessert at dinner or luncheon.

APPLE SPONGE PUDDING—One cup of sifted pastry flour and sift it with one level teaspoon of baking powder. Beat the yolks of three eggs until light colored, add one cup of sugar and the juice of one lemon. Fold in the stiffly beaten whites of the three eggs and then the flour. Spread the batter thinly on a large shallow pan and bake about twenty minutes in a moderate oven. Turn out of the pan, trim off any hard edges, spread with stewed, sweetened, and flavored apples, and roll up at once like a jelly roll. Serve with a liquid sauce or a syrup made from sugar and water.

APRICOT KISSES—Beat the whites of two eggs until very light and still, flavor with one-half teaspoon vanilla and then carefully fold in one cup of fine granulated sugar. Lay a sheet of paraffin paper over the bottom of a large baking pan and drop the mixture on the paper, in any size you wish from one teaspoon to two tablespoons. Have them some distance apart so they will not run together. Bake them in a very moderate oven and be careful to bake sufficiently, say forty-five minutes. They should be only delicately colored and yet dry all through. When done remove to a platter and break the top in, remove a little of the inside and fill pulp of sifted peaches, sweetened and mixed with equal parts of whipped cream. Sprinkle pistachio nuts over the top and serve fancy cakes.

BAKED CUSTARD—Beat four eggs, whites and yolks together lightly, and add a quart of milk, four tablespoons sugar, a pinch of salt and flavoring. Bake in stoneware cups or a shallow bowl, set in a pan of water.

BAKED BANANAS, PORTO RICAN FASHION—Select rather green bananas, put them, without removing the skins, into hot ashes or a very hot oven and bake until the skins burst open. Send to the table in a folded napkin. The skins help hold in the heat and are not to be removed until the moment of eating. Serve plenty of butter with them.

BANANA AND LEMON JELLY CREAM—Soak one-half box of gelatin in one cup of cold water. Shave the rind of one lemon, using none of the white, and steep it with one square inch stick of cinnamon in one pint of boiling water ten minutes. Add the soaked gelatin, one cup of sugar and three-fourths of a cup of lemon juice, and when dissolved strain into shallow dishes. When cold cut it in dice or break it up with a fork, and put it in a glass dish in layers with spiced bananas. Pour a cold boiled custard over them and cover with a meringue. Brown the meringue on a plate and slip it off over the custard.

CUSTARD PUDDING—Line a baking dish with slices of sponge cake. Make a boiled custard with four cups of milk and the yolks of five eggs, one-half cup of sugar and flavored with vanilla. Pour the custard into the baking-dish. Beat the whites of the eggs to a stiff froth with one-half cup of powdered sugar and spread over the top. Set in a very slow oven to brown slightly.

CUSTARD SOUFFLE—Mix one-fourth cup of sugar, one cup flour and one cup of cold milk. Stir till it thickens, add one-fourth cup of butter, cool, stir in the beaten yolks of four eggs and then the stiffly beaten whites. Turn into a buttered shallow dish, set in a pan of hot water and bake in a moderate oven half an hour. Serve at once.

FIG AND RHUBARB—Wash two bunches of rhubarb and cut into inch pieces without peeling. Put into boiler with a cupful sugar and four or five figs cut in inch pieces. Put on the cover and cook over hot water until the rhubarb is tender and the syrup is rich and jelly-like in consistency. Raisins are nice cooked in rhubarb the same way. If preferred, and you are to have a hot oven anyway, put the rhubarb and figs or raisins in a stone pot, cover closely and bake in the oven until jellied.

COLD RHUBARB DESSERT—Peel tender stalks and cut enough into half-inch pieces to measure two cups. Cook with one cup of water, the grated rind from a large orange and two cups of sugar. Do not stir while cooking, but lift from the range now and then to prevent burning. When soft but not broken, add two and one-half tablespoons of gelatin soaked fifteen minutes in one-half cup of cold water. Stir with a fork just enough to mix and pour all into a large mold. When formed, unmold, and serve with cream.

GERMAN DESSERT—Beat two eggs and a pinch of salt, add two cupfuls of milk and pour into a deep plate. Soak slices of bread in this, one at a time until softened, but not enough to break. Melt a rounding tablespoon of butter in a pan and in this brown the bread on both sides. Serve with an orange pudding sauce or any kind of liquid sauce preferred.

LEMON SPONGE—Soak one-half box of gelatin in one-half cup of cold water. Add the juice of four lemons to one cup of sugar, then the beaten yolks of four eggs, add two cups of cold water, and bring to a boiling point. Stir in the soaked gela-tin and strain into a large bowl set in a pan of ice. Beat now and then until it begins to harden, then add the unbeaten whites of four eggs and beat continuously until the sponge is light and firm. Fill into molds before the sponge is too hard to form into the shape of the mold.

MOSAIC JELLY—One and one-half cups of milk, two level tablespoons sugar, rind of one-half lemon, one-half bay-leaf, one level tablespoon granulated gelatin, one-fourth cup of water, yolks two eggs. Scald the milk with the sugar, lemon rind, and bay-leaf, then add the gelatin soaked in water for twenty minutes. Stir until dissolved and strain the hot mixture gradually into the egg yolks slightly beaten. Return to double boiler and stir until thickened. Remove from fire and color one-half of the mixture either pink or green, and turn each half into a shallow pan wet with cold water. When cold cut into squares or oblongs. Line a mold with lemon jelly and garnish with the colored pieces. Add the remaining jelly, chill thoroughly and serve on a platter garnished with whipped cream.

PINEAPPLE BAVARIAN CREAM—Grate enough pineapple to make two cups. Soak two level teaspoons of gelatin in one-half cup of cold water for twenty minutes. Heat the pineapple to the scalding point, add the soaked gelatin and stir until dissolved, then add one-third cup sugar, stir and fold in three cups of beaten cream. Turn into molds and chill.

SCALLOPED APPLE—Measure two even cups of fine breadcrumbs and pour over them one-quarter cup of melted butter. Mix two rounding tablespoons of sugar with the grated yellow rind and the juice of one lemon and four gratings of nutmeg. Butter a baking dish, scatter in some crumbs, put in one pint of pared, cored and sliced apples, scatter on one-half of the seasoning, another pint of apples, the remainder of the seasoning and cover with the last of the crumbs. Put a cover on the dish and bake twenty minutes, uncover and bake twenty minutes longer.

SPANISH CREAM—Put one and two-thirds teaspoons of gelatin into one-third cup of cold water. Heat two cups of milk in a double boiler, add the yolks of two eggs, beaten with one-half cup of sugar until light, and when the custard thickens take from stove and set in pan of cold water. Beat the whites of two eggs until stiff, and dissolve the soaked gelatin in three-quarters cup of boiling water. When the custard is cool, add a teaspoon of vanilla, the strained gelatin and the whites of the eggs beaten stiff. Stir all together lightly and turn into mold.

STEAMED PUDDING—Beat one-half cup of butter with one cup of sugar to a cream, add two beaten eggs and cup of flour sifted with one teaspoon each of cinnamon and soda, two cups of breadcrumbs, soaked in one cup of sour milk. Add one cup of chopped and seeded raisins and one-half cup of chopped dates. Steam two hours and serve with whipped cream.

STRAWBERRY SARABANDE—Whip a cupful thick cream until very stiff, then fold carefully into it a pint of fresh berries cut in small pieces with a silver knife. Have ready a tablespoonful gelatin soaked in a quarter cup cold water for half an hour, then dissolved by setting the cup containing it in hot water. Add by degrees to the berries and cream, whipping it in so that it will not string. Add three tablespoonfuls powdered sugar and when it stiffens turn into a cold mold and set on the ice. When ready to serve turn out onto a pretty dessert platter.

WALNUT SUNDAE—Put one cone of vanilla ice cream in a sherbet cup, or better yet in a champagne glass and sprinkle with minced walnuts.

YORKSHIRE PUDDING—Take an equal number of eggs and tablespoonful of sifted flour, and when the eggs are well beaten mix them in with the flour, add some salt and a little grated nutmeg, and then pour in as much new milk as will make a batter of the consistency of cream, serve the batter with a fork well for ten minutes and then put in at once into a baking tin, which must be very hot, containing a couple of tablespoons of hot drippings. Set the pudding in oven to bake or before the fire under the roasting meat. When ready to serve cut the pudding into squares and send to the table on a separate dish.

APPLE PUDDING—Butter a pudding dish and line it with slices of toasted stale bread buttered and wet with milk. Over these put a thick layer of peeled, cored, and sliced tart apples, and sprinkle generously with granulated sugar and cinnamon or nutmeg. Over these put a cover of more toast buttered, moistened and sprinkled with sugar. Cover with a plate and bake for two hours in a moderate oven, taking off the plate toward the last that the top may brown. Serve with maple or other syrup for sauce.

APPLE PUDDING—Four cups flour, one level teaspoon salt, six level teaspoons baking powder, four level tablespoons butter, two cups milk, two cups finely chopped apple, one-half cup butter, two cups sugar, one and one-half quarts water. Sift together the flour, salt, and baking powder. Work in the butter with the fingers and add the milk. Mix well, turn onto floured board, roll out one-half inch thick, cover with the apple and roll up like a jelly roll. Press the ends together and press down the side, to keep the apple in. Place in a buttered pan and add the butter, sugar and water. Bake in a moderate oven for one and one-half hours.

APPLE SPONGE PUDDING—One cup of sifted pastry flour and one level teaspoon of baking powder. Beat the yolks of three eggs until light colored, add one cup of sugar and the juice of one lemon. Fold in the stiffly beaten whites of the three eggs and then the flour. Spread the batter thinly on a large shallow pan and bake about twenty minutes in a moderate oven. Turn out of the pan, trim off any hard edges, spread with stewed sweetened and flavored apples, and roll up at once like a jelly roll. Serve with a liquid sauce or a syrup of sugar and water.

BAKED CHERRY PUDDING—Cream one-quarter cup of butter with one-half cup of sugar, add the yolks of two eggs beaten very light, two cups of milk, two cups of flour sifted twice with four level teaspoons of baking powder, and last, the whites of the eggs beaten stiff. Stone cherries to measure three cups, drain off the juice and put them into a pudding dish.

BAKED PUDDING—Stir one-half cup of flour smooth in one cup of cold milk, add two unbeaten eggs and beat several minutes, then add one cup more of milk and a saltspoon of salt. Stir together, pour into a buttered baking dish and set directly into the oven. Serve with lemon thickened sauce.

COCOA RICE MERINGUE—Beat one pint of milk, add one-quarter cup of washed rice and a saltspoon of salt. Cook until tender. Add one level tablespoon of butter, one-half cup of seeded raisins, half a teaspoon of vanilla, and one slightly rounding tablespoon of cocoa, cook five minutes. Fold in the stiffly beaten whites of two eggs and one-half cup of beaten cream. Turn into a buttered baking dish, cover with the whites of three eggs beaten stiff, with one-third cup of powdered sugar and a level tablespoon of cocoa. Set in a moderate oven for a few minutes until the meringue is cooked.

COTTAGE PUDDING—Beat the yolk of one egg, add one cup of granulated sugar, one-half cup of milk, one and one-half cups of flour in two spoons of baking powder, stir in the white of one egg beaten stiff. Bake in a moderate oven.

CRANBERRY AND CUSTARD PUDDING—Here is a new suggestion which comes from a high authority. Take one sugar cooky or four lady fingers, if you have them, and crumble into a baking dish. Cover with a thin layer of cranberry preserves or jelly, dot with small lumps of butter and add a sprinkle of cinnamon. Beat three eggs (separately) very lightly, add two tablespoonfuls of sugar and two cupfuls of milk. Pour over the fruit and cake, bake as a custard and serve with whipped cream.

CUSTARD PUDDING—Line a baking dish with slices of sponge cake. Make a boiled custard with four cups of milk and the yolks of five eggs, one-half cup of sugar, and flavored with vanilla. Pour the custard into the baking dish. Beat the whites of the eggs to a stiff froth with one-half cup of powdered sugar and spread over the top. Set in a very slow oven to brown slightly.

DATE MERINGUE—Beat the whites of five eggs until stiff, add three rounding tablespoons of powdered sugar, and beat again. Add a teaspoon of lemon juice and a half a pound of stoned and chopped dates. Turn into a buttered baking dish and bake fifteen minutes in a moderate oven. Serve with a boiled custard.

EGG SOUFFLE—Make a sauce from one cup of hot milk and two level tablespoons each of butter and flour, cooked together five minutes in a double boiler. Add the yolks of four eggs beaten well, stir enough to mix well and remove from the fire. Add half a level teaspoon of salt and a few grains of cayenne. Fold in the whites of the eggs beaten stiff, turn into a buttered dish, set in a pan of hot water, and bake in a slow oven until firm. Serve in the same dish.

FRUIT PUDDING—One and one-half cups flour, two and one-half cups raisins, one-half cup molasses, one-half cup milk, two tablespoons butter, one teaspoon cinnamon, one-half tea-spoon allspice, one-half teaspoon nutmeg, one-half teaspoon salt, mix all together, one-half teaspoon soda, dissolved in hot water, steam two hours. Hard or liquid sauce, or both.

INDIAN TAPIOCA PUDDING—One-third cup tapioca, one-fourth cup cornmeal, one quart scalded milk, half cup molasses, two tablespoons butter, one-half teaspoon salt, one teaspoon ginger and cinnamon mixed, one cup cold milk. Soak the tapioca in cold water for one hour, then drain. Pour the hot milk on to the cornmeal gradually. Add the tapioca and cook in double boiler until transparent. Add molasses, butter, salt, and spice, and turn into a buttered baking dish. Pour the cold milk over the top and bake for one hour in a moderate oven.

LEMON MERINGUE PUDDING—Soak one cup of fine breadcrumbs in two cups of milk until soft. Beat one-quarter cup of butter and one-half of sugar together until greasy, stir all into the milk and crumbs. Grate a little yellow lemon peel over the top and pour into a buttered baking dish. Set in a moderate oven until firm and slightly browned. Make a meringue of the stiffly beaten whites of two eggs and four level tablespoons of powdered sugar. Spread over the pudding, return to the oven and color a little.

LEMON PUDDING—Three eggs, one scant cup sugar, one lemon juice and rind, two cups of milk, two liberal tablespoons cornstarch, one heaping teaspoon butter. Scald the milk and stir in the cornstarch, stirring all the time until it thickens well, add the butter and set aside to cool. When cool beat the eggs light, add sugar, the lemon juice and grated rind, and whip in a great spoonful at a time, the stiffened cornstarch and milk. Bake in a buttered dish and eat cold.

LITTLE STEAMED PUDDING—Cream one-quarter cup butter with one-half cup of sugar, add one-quarter cup milk, then one cup of flour sifted with two teaspoons of baking powder and a pinch of salt, and last fold in the stiffly beaten whites of three eggs. Have some small molds or cups buttered, fill half full with the batter, cover with buttered paper, and steam three-quarters of an hour. Serve hot with a sauce.

NEW HAMPSHIRE INDIAN MEAL PUDDING—Bring a quart of milk to a boil, then sprinkle in slowly about a cup and a quarter of yellow meal, stirring constantly. (An exact rule for the meal cannot be given, as some swells more than others.) As soon as the milk is thickened take from the fire and cool slightly before adding three-quarters of a cup of molasses, half a teaspoonful salt and a tablespoonful ginger. Beat the mixture until smooth, and lastly turn in a quart of cold milk, stirring very little. Pour into a well greased pudding dish and set in a very slow oven. This pudding needs about five hours of very slow baking to insure its becoming creamy, instead of hard and lumpy. The batter, after the cold milk is added should be about the consistency of pancake batter. Serve with cream or maple syrup.

ORANGE PUDDING—Take one cup of fine stale bread-crumbs, not dried, and moisten them with as much milk as they will absorb and become thoroughly softened. Beat the yolks of four eggs with the whites of two, add four tablespoons of sugar and the grated peel of one orange, using of course only the outer cells. Stir this into the softened crumbs, then beat the other two whites until stiff and fold them into the mixture. Turn it into a well buttered mold and steam it two hours. Turn out into a hot dish and serve with orange sauce.

PEACH TAPIOCA—Prepare a dish of tapioca in the usual way, into a buttered pudding dish put a layer of cooked and sweetened tapioca, then a layer of peaches, fresh or canned. Next add another layer of tapioca, then more peaches, and so on until the dish is full. Flavor with lemon and sprinkle three-fourths of a cup of sugar over all, then bake in a very hot oven until a light brown.

RASPBERRY DUMPLINGS—Wash one cup of rice and put into the double boiler. Pour over it two cups of boiling water, add one-half teaspoon of salt and two tablespoons of sugar and cook thirty minutes or until soft. Have some small pudding cloths about twelve inches square, wring them out of hot water and lay them over a small half pint bowl. Spread the rice one-third of an inch thick over the cloth, and fill the center with fresh raspberries. Draw the cloth around until the rice covers the berries and they are good round shape. Tie the ends of the cloth firmly, drop them into boiling water and cook twenty min-utes. Remove the cloth and serve with lemon sauce.

SPOON PUDDING—Cream one tablespoonful butter with two tablespoonfuls sugar. Add two tablespoonfuls flour, pinch of salt, one tablespoonful cornstarch, beaten yolk of one egg and tablespoonful of cream. Beat well, and lastly add beaten white of egg and one teaspoonful baking powder. Pour over berries and steam forty minutes. Serve with whipped cream.

SQUASH PUDDING—One pint of finely mashed cooked squash, one cup of sugar, one teaspoon of ground cinnamon, a little salt, the juice and grated rind of one lemon, add slowly one quart of boiling milk, stirring well, and when a little cooled, add five well beaten eggs. Bake in a pudding dish set in a pan of hot water, in a moderate oven, until firm in the center. Serve with cream.

STEAMED BERRY PUDDING—Sift two cups of flour with four teaspoons of baking powder, rub in a rounding tablespoon of butter, add two beaten eggs, one cup of milk, one-half cup of sugar, and last two cups of blueberries. The berries should be rinsed in cold water, shaken in a cheese cloth until dry and then rolled in flour before adding. Pour into a pudding mold, and steam one and one-quarter hours. Serve with liquid sauce.

STEAMED PUDDING—Beat one-half cup of butter with one cup of sugar to a cream, add two beaten eggs and cup of flour sifted with one teaspoon each of cinnamon and soda, two cups of breadcrumbs, soaked in one cup of sour milk. Add one cup of chopped and seeded raisins and one-half cup of chopped dates. Steam two hours and serve with whipped cream.

TAPIOCA MERINGUE—Soak one-half cup granulated tapi-oca in a pint of cold water for half an hour. Cook slowly twenty minutes until transparent. If too thick, add a little more boiling water. Boil one quart of milk in a farina kettle with a pinch of salt and the yellow rind of half lemon. Beat the yolks of four eggs with a cup of sugar, add slowly to the milk, stirring until smooth and creamy, but do not allow it to boil. When thickened, remove from the fire, add a teaspoonful flavoring and blend thoroughly. Whip the whites of the eggs to a stiff froth with three tablespoonfuls powdered sugar and a teaspoonful flavoring, spread over the top of the pudding which should have been poured in the serving dish and set in a coolish oven to puff and color a golden yellow.

TAPIOCA PUDDING—Cover one cup of the flake tapioca with cold water and let it stand two hours. Stir occasionally with a fork to separate the lumps. Put in a farina kettle with a pint and a half water.

Slice three tart apples and put in with the tapioca, together with sugar to sweeten to taste. Stir all together and cook until the apples are soft and the tapioca clear. Serve hot or cold. Peaches may be used in place of the apple. Serve with cream.

TAPIOCA SOUFFLE—Soak three tablespoonfuls pearl tapioca in water to cover for three or four hours. Then add a quart of milk and cook until the tapioca is perfectly clear and the milk thickened. It will take about twenty minutes, and unless you use the farina kettle, must be stirred constantly. Add the yolks of four eggs beaten with two-thirds cup sugar and cook two or three minutes, stirring steadily. Whip the whites of four eggs to a stiff froth, fold through the cooked cream, and take directly from the fire. Flavor with lemon or vanilla and bake in a moderate oven for twenty-five minutes. Chill and serve. This may also be served as a pudding without the final baking.

WHOLE WHEAT PUDDING—Put one cup of milk, one-half cup of molasses, two cups of graham or whole wheat flour, one cup of chopped raisins and half a saltspoon of salt into a bowl and add one level teaspoon of soda, dissolved in a tablespoon of warm water, beat hard for three minutes. Pour the thin batter into a buttered pudding mold and steam two and a half hours. Serve with a lemon sauce or cream.

YORKSHIRE PUDDING—Take an equal number of eggs and tablespoonful of sifted flour and when the eggs are well beaten mix them in with the flour, add some salt and a little grated nutmeg and then pour in as much new milk as will make a batter of the consistency of cream, serve the batter with a fork well for ten minutes and then put in at once into a baking tin which must be very hot, containing a couple of tablespoons of hot drippings. Set the pudding in oven to bake or before the fire under the roasting meat. When ready to serve cut the pudding into squares and send to the table on a separate dish.

If You Like Cocoa
This Will Captivate You

ZATEK
(ZAY-TECK)
COCOA

Everybody who drinks ZATEK Cocoa knows that its unusually delicious flavor sets it apart from all others.

ZATEK Cocoa is the very finest that skill and science can produce, yet it is not the most expensive.

Order ZATEK Cocoa from your grocer today. Give each of the family a steaming cup for dinner tonight. They're sure to note the difference in flavor and taste.

ZATEK Cocoa is packed in pound, half-pound and ten-cent tins. Keep a package always handy. It is the most economical, delicious and strengthening beverage your family can drink.

PENNSYLVANIA CHOCOLATE COMPANY   Pittsburgh, U. S. A.

ZATEK COCOA AD FROM 1916.

FOOD CRATE LABEL FROM THE 1920S.
NOTE THE PAPER-WRAPPED ORANGE
IN THE BOTTOM LEFT CORNER.

SAUCE FOR PUDDINGS

FRUIT SYRUP SAUCE—One cup fruit syrup, one-half cup sugar, one teaspoon butter. Use the syrup from apricots, peaches, cherries, quinces or any fruit you prefer. The amount of sugar will depend upon the acidity of the fruit. Mix the corn-starch with the sugar, add the syrup and boil all together five minutes. Add the butter last.

LEMON SAUCE—Grate the rind and squeeze the juice of one lemon. Mix together three teaspoons cornstarch, one cup of sugar and two cups of boiling water, and cook ten minutes, stirring constantly. Add the lemon rind and juice and one teaspoon of butter.

LEMON SAUCE—Mix three dessert spoons of cornstarch with one cup of sugar, pinch of salt, in a saucepan, pour on two cups boiling water and stir quickly as it thickens. When it is smooth set it back where it will simply bubble and simmer, and stir occasionally. Add the grated rind and juice of one lemon and one rounding tablespoon butter. If this is too thick add more hot water as it thickens in cooling, and you want it thin enough to pour easily.

LEMON SAUCE—Mix three tablespoons of cornstarch with one cup of cold water and turn on one cup of boiling water. Boil ten minutes, then add one cup of sugar, the juice and grated yellow rind of one lemon and two rounding tablespoons of butter.

LEMON SAUCE FOR FRITTERS—Mix four level teaspoons of cornstarch with one cup of sugar, and stir at once into two cups of boiling water, add the juice and grated yellow rind of one lemon and cook six minutes, add three level tablespoons of butter.

ORANGE SAUCE No. 1—Mix one and a half tablespoons of cornstarch with one cup of sugar, and stir it into one pint of boiling water. Let it cook quickly and stir as it thickens, and after ten minutes add two tablespoons of butter and one-half cup of orange juice. Cook two minutes longer, then serve.

ORANGE SAUCE No. 2—Chip the yellow rind from an orange and squeeze the juice over it. Let stand half an hour. Stir one-quarter cup of flour into one cup of sugar and turn into two cups of boiling water. Cook ten minutes, add a pinch of salt, the orange rind and juice, stir and strain.

RASPBERRY SAUCE FOR ICE CREAM—If you think that a good ice cream is yet not quite fine enough, pour a raspberry sauce over each portion as served. Add one-quarter cup of sugar to one cup of raspberry juice prepared as for jelly-making, and simmer five minutes. Add a rounding teaspoon of arrow-root made smooth in one tablespoon of cold water, and cook five minutes. Now add one tablespoon of strained lemon juice and let boil up once.

SAUCE FOR CHERRY PUDDING—Put two cups of cherry juice, or juice and water, into a saucepan, stir in three level tablespoons of cornstarch and cook fifteen minutes. Add two-thirds cup of sugar and a tablespoon of lemon juice.

SAUCE FOR BATTER PUDDING—Beat together in a bowl three rounding tablespoons of sugar, two level tablespoons of butter and one of flour. When the mixture is white add one-half cup of boiling water and stir until all is well melted. Add a little lemon juice and serve.

SAUCE FOR PUDDINGS—Beat the whites of three eggs until stiff, add one-half cup powdered sugar and the grated yellow rind of half a lemon. Pour on slowly one cup of boiling water, stirring all the time and the sauce is ready to serve.

STRAWBERRY SAUCE—Beat together one-half cupful of butter and a cup of sugar until white and light. The success of this sauce depends upon the long beating. Add to the creamed butter and sugar the stiffly whipped white of an egg and a cupful of strawberries mashed to a pulp.

DRINK
"BLACK DIAMOND" WHISKEY
RICH and MELLOW

COBLENTZ & LEVY
PORTLAND, OREGON

RARE ADVERTISEMENT FOR BLACK DIAMOND WHISKEY
FROM THE LATE 1800S.

Illustration by Steve Quinn

FOOD TRADING CARDS OF THE LATE 1800S AND EARLY 1900S
ENCOURAGED THE PURCHASE OF THEIR PRODUCT.
HERE, LION COFFEE PROMISES "A BEAUTIFUL PICTURE CARD IN
EVERY PACKAGE." THE BACK OF THE CARD DELIVERS, AS PROMISED,
WITH THIS LOVELY PASTEL OF CHILDREN PLAYING ALONG A RIVER.

BEVERAGES

COCOA WITH WHIPPED CREAM—Heat four cups of milk to the scalding point over hot water, or in a double boiler. Milk should be heated by direct contact with the fire. Mix a few grains of salt, three level tablespoons of cocoa and one-fourth cup of sugar to a paste with a little of the milk. then add three-fourths cup of boiling water and boil one minute, add to the hot milk and beat two minutes by the clock. Serve with a tablespoon of beaten or whipped cream on top of each cup.

CURRANT JULEP—Pick over currants and measure two cups. Mash them and pour on two cups of cold water. Strain and chill the juice. Put one tablespoon of simple syrup in a tall glass, add three bruised fresh mint leaves and fill with the currant juice. Add three or four perfect raspberries and serve. The syrup is made by simmering for twenty minutes, one cup of sugar and two of water.

CURRANT SHRUB—Pick over and mash two quarts of ripe currants, add one pint of vinegar, and let stand over night. Set on the range and bring to the boiling point, then strain twice. Measure the clear liquid, and allow one cup of sugar to each cup of liquid. Simmer twenty minutes and seal in bottles.

RASPBERRY SHRUB—Put one quart of ripe raspberries in a bowl, add two cups of vinegar, mash the berries slightly, and let stand over night. In the morning, scald and strain until clear. Measure, and to each cup of juice add one cup of sugar, boil twenty minutes and seal.

STRAWBERRY SYRUP—Pick over, rinse, drain and remove the hulls from several quarts of ripe berries. Fill a porcelain lined double boiler with the fruit and set it over the lower boiler half full of boiling water, and let it heat until the juice flows freely. Mash the berries, then turn out into a cloth strainer and cook the remainder of the fruit in the same way. When all the juice is pressed out, measure it and allow an equal amount of sugar. Let the juice come to the boiling point, add the sugar and cook five minutes from the time the whole begins to boil. Turn into jars or bottles and seal the same as canned fruit. This is excellent for beverages, flavoring ice cream and other fancy creams, and will be found desirable for many purposes when fresh fruit is not at hand.

ADDITIONAL RECIPES

TABLE OF CONTENTS

137

ORIGINALLY
Designed, Engraved *and* Printed
by The Franklin Company, Chicago

FRONT COVER FROM 1882'S *Minstrel and Plantation Songs.*
INSIDE, PIANO MUSIC INCLUDES "WORLD-WIDE FAMOUS"
MINSTREL SONGS, PLANTATION SONGS, AND
"THE MOST POPULAR OF THE CELEBRATED" MELODIES FROM THE
FIRST PROFESSIONAL AMERICAN MUSIC WRITER AND COMPOSER,
STEPHEN COLLINS FOSTER (1826-1864).

A SOUTHERN BAPTISM 1900-1906
Photograph courtesy of the Library of Congress